THEORIZING *f*EMINISM

Gender

Also in the series

Gendering Caste
Uma Chakravarti

Patriarchy
Gail Omvedt and V. Geetha

Interrogating Motherhood
Jasodhara Bagchi

THEORIZING *f*EMINISM

series editor Maithreyi Krishnaraj

Gender

V. Geetha

Stree

GENDER was first published in January 2002
by STREE, an imprint of Bhatkal and Sen,
16 Southern Avenue, Calcutta 700 026

First reprint August 2006
Second reprint November 2009
Third reprint May 2012
Fourth reprint 2015
Fifth reprint 2017
Sixth reprint 2021
Seventh reprint 2023
Eighth reprint 2024

ISBN 81-85604-45-2

Rs 500

Typesetting by Sonal Mansata,
87K Park St, Calcutta 700 016.
Printed at Sarat Impressions Pvt Ltd
18B Shyama Charan De Street, Kolkata 700073

Printed by Mandira Sen for STREE,
an imprint of Bhatkal and Sen
16 Southern Avenue, Calcutta 700 026

For Nayreh Tohidi,
wherever you are

Foreword

THEORIZING FEMINISM IN INDIA

The idea for this series came from many teachers in our colleges and other higher institutions. They constantly complained that they did not know what to use for teaching women's studies to beginners. Not that there was any dearth of material. Women's studies had become a publishing success. The problem was that it was so uneven in quality. An abundance of books from the West thanks to their superior distribution channels flood our markets. Every research report or dissertation of every minor or major university, sooner or later, is hastily pushed between the covers of a published volume, filling our libraries, extending the résumés of teachers and lining the pockets of the publishing industry. Under the sheer weight of detail on local specifics of these dissertations or funded research projects, theory or analysis are stifled. What does one choose? Many years ago I had launched an experimental 'feminist concepts' working papers from the centre where I worked, which found a ready audience and those papers were much in demand. There was a suggestion, three or four years ago by Sujata Patel that updating them would be a signal service. Mandira Sen of Stree, Calcutta, came forward to support such a venture, a series of book on 'concepts' in a popular, jargon free mode, where ideas would be explained in a lucid readable style. We sorely lack this kind of material in this country. We have either learned treatises on the one hand and racy, superficial journalist writing on the other with nothing in between. The success of any social reform depends on effective communication to the public by making difficult ideas easy. It seemed though restrictive to think only of 'concepts'. So, the idea got expanded into working out a broader theme of 'theorizing' on a range of issues. It has taken some time before we were able to actually launch this. We wrote to more than two dozen women's studies scholars who have made signal contributions, eliciting their cooperation. They were expected to write on topics or areas they had pursued vigourously over the years. The series can also serve as an invitation to other young scholars to launch similar efforts and attempt new themes.

Students and teachers would readily agree that the position of women in our society is an unequal one but they also take for granted what exists and have difficulty in penetrating beyond this taken-for-grantedness of everyday phenomena. Women's studies being something new, many teachers do not have a familiarity with its perspective and content.

It is now more than two decades since formal women's studies centres or departments became established within universities. While women's studies may be located in a particular faculty, the content and approach of women's studies is inevitably interdisciplinary. Even now there is more research than teaching in women's studies. In the last few years, selections edited by well-known scholars have been coming out regularly. These to some extent fill the gap in curricula. However, these are meant only for the specialized readers, mainly university students, and draw upon published articles in learned journals. Social activists confronted with many learned tomes cannot figure out how they can translate these theories into their practice or use them to understand the day-to-day problems. 'Theories' seem so abstract, so remote, fascinating, yes, but where exactly do these lead them in their quest for making sense of problems or in evolving strategies? Not just action groups but ordinary women coping with their daily struggles want to know what they can do. For instance, we have theories to offer about sexual division of labour in society and what it does. However we find that our action agenda is unable to dislodge this. Why? There are many single men in the West (and may be, here too) who do housework—cook, clean—or single fathers who care for children, but within marriage such a reallocation of gender-specific tasks is extremely hard. Another tricky area is the family.

The woman or man in the street is frankly put off either by the academic jargon or misses the thrust of the arguments. No term has been so much misunderstood or maligned and shunned as 'feminism'. Some of us who were 'doing' women's studies felt it was our duty to bring to a larger public the richness and scope of the intellectual effort of women' studies to locating, understanding, explaining problems connected with the relationship of men and women, of women to each other and of both to society and social institutions in general so that we may be able to find solutions. There is a history behind the problems we face now as well as a history in the way we perceived issues. Much of theorizing therefore takes the form of a search into the past to see how it led to the present. This is not such a simple matter. Interpreting the past, filling in gaps, making surmises where evidence is hard to come by, relating it to the present—this is not easy and requires a great deal of information on related aspects of society, culture, economics and politics.

Contributions to enrich our knowledge has come from many quarters—men committed to emancipation of women, scholars, men and women, women's action groups, legal practitioners, creative writers, artists, journalists and social workers. It is out of this fertilization that theorizing began to emerge. Today women's studies has acquired sufficient legitimacy if not parity, with other disciplines. Women's studies has evolved its own distinct vocabulary, conceptual tools, analytical frameworks and problematiques. It has generated theories, posed critical questions and identified for serious inquiry concerns of import to all of us, if indeed we wish to make human living a better deal for all of us on this planet. It has tackled many perennial issues that afflict human society such as the causes of women's subordination and ways to end it and in so doing has permeated our thinking, penetrated many disciplines and altered our views on human nature, philosophies, language, literature, art, and the natural, social and behavioural sciences.

This series aims at publishing introductory texts for readers outside academia as well as for those inside it. Written by well-known scholar-activists of women's studies, the books seek to explain ideas and theories in a simple way and to place them securely in the Indian context. Each reviews an area or theme, drawing from both feminist theory and categories in general, and the specific Indian experience, to bring out the context-determined outcomes. Many feminist theories originated in the West and therefore reflected the social and cultural background of the writers and the nature of social configurations within which they sought explanations. Dominant features like the nuclear family, advanced capitalism, different marriage patterns and cultural ethos naturally shape these scholars' understanding of women in society. In the beginning, they too omitted race. More relevant for us are the extended family and its hold over loyalties of members, an economy in transition to capitalism, a deeply hierarchic society stratified by class and caste, and persistent religious differences. Scholars here have used standard feminist theories in innovative and imaginative ways, modifying them, elaborating them and offering us a comparative perspective. Thus a very important aim of the series is to bring together this contribution of Third World feminism and feminist theorizing in the broad sense of conceptualizing social reality. The emergence of autonomous grass-root women's movements here, have forced us to rethink our views on liberation and questions of who speaks for whom. It has brought to the forefront a fundamental dilemma—we began by a strong notion of universal sisterhood and now we realize there are divergent interests among us. How do we reconcile them? From saying we are tied by a common bond of oppression to saying we do not have the same kind of oppression, does it leave us stranded in theory?

Each book is meant to be self-sufficient in itself and yet cumulatively add to the theory building. As each is written by a different author, the style will vary. There would be overlaps but this should not matter. The constituent essays in the series are not repetitive but additive. We hope these books will be used widely not as 'prescribed texts' to be memorized for examinations but for debate and discussion in the classroom and outside; as a spring board for further thought and not as congealed wisdom. We hope to get these translated into regional languages so that the purpose of wider dissemination and of provoking discussion will be better served. The series can serve as an invitation to other scholars who were not part of the team to launch similar efforts; attempt new themes. There is an endless scope for educating ourselves. In the quick and easy recipes of 'gender awareness' programmes, what is missed is that behaviour change occurs never by rhetoric but only when there is a clear understanding of what the limitations and possibilities are, for gaining one's freedom in the present situation. One woman who attended a women's studies course dropped out, she said, because the course only made her suffering more acute by knowing about it. She was pointing out the shortcoming in the manner of our outreach. We hold to a vision, project an ideal because that is what gives a direction but that does not mean it can be achieved now or in the near future. One does not therefore give up the struggle or give up courage.

We hope this series helps in the kind of understanding of everyday life that gives one the incentive to explore more, to ask new questions all the time. V. Geetha's essay on gender is the first in our series. We thank her for the dedication and effort she has imparted to our enterprise.

Series Editor
Mumbai, Oct 2001 MAITHREYI KRISHNARAJ

Preface

Gender is everywhere. When we dress a girl child in soft colours and frilly clothes, buy a male child a gun, when we admonish girls for behaving like boys, or tease boys for being timid 'like girls', we are 'doing' gender. That is, we are allocating to the male and female sexes specific and distinctive attributes and roles; likewise, we also impose different sets of expectations on them. More important, we seem to imply that these attributes and roles may not be easily exchanged. We do all of this without much thought, are not particularly self-conscious about thus ordering the world. In other words, it appears fairly commonsensical to us that boys and girls ought to be distinguished through physical markers such as clothes, that they behave differently, are raised to different things. If questioned, we answer that this is natural, the way things are and have always been, that God or Nature intended us to live thus.

In our lives, however, we seldom remain tied to those roles, qualities and behaviour patterns, which are expected of us. While the facts of our sex—the presence of distinctive male and female genitalia and reproductive organs—are incontrovertible, the things we are meant to do, or the ways we are meant to be, are not. A girl often feels frustrated when she finds out that she can be neither patient or tolerant—qualities which women are supposed to possess in abundance. She may not be passive either, willing to sit things out on the sidelines.

Likewise, there are young men who feel uncomfortable having to prove, insistently and unhappily, that they are macho. These men probably dislike fast bikes, do not want to tease girls, nor do they feel that the world is theirs to appropriate and own. Such young men are bound to feel uneasy with the shadowy ideal of a powerful and authoritative masculinity that looms large over them.

Then again, many of us feel that the ordering of the world, and human behaviour into masculine and feminine is unfair. Women, of course, and with good reason, are more likely to feel thus—even the wealthiest and most powerful of women are perceived chiefly as mothers, wives, daughters or sisters. They are seldom viewed as persons in their own right and very few women see themselves as autonomous beings. Some men too experience the world they find themselves in as being deeply discriminatory because they are subject to norms that elevate some men over all men and women. Other men feel that they are less evolved than women, in matters of emotional happiness and pleasure, and therefore imagine that women are better off than them. Men, they say with sorrow cannot be loving, nurturing and self-sacrificing as women can be.

The point is, at various moments in our lives we do actively question routine practices of gender. But we rarely question the fundamental premises on which these practices are based. We do not ask ourselves whether men and women are not more similar than we imagine them to be. Whether masculine and feminine attributes and roles cannot be exchanged or transformed, or what if men and women can be equal to and coeval with each other.

To make sense of gender, we need to look at our lives closely and critically. Why are people expected to be exclusively masculine or feminine? We need to examine the ways in which women have been rendered subordinate to men. Equally we must understand the nature and details of male authority. How do men experience it? We need to ask ourselves whether there is anything 'normal' about our world being arranged this way, and if there are other ways of arranging it.

This is just what we will discuss in this book. It begins with a description of the commonplace interpretations of the term 'gender'. It then goes on to suggest that gender is both a part of the world we live in, as well as a way of understanding that world. Chapters 2-4 present descriptions of some of the more well-known and persuasive arguments about masculine and feminine natures, characters, roles and destinies. Chapter 5 offers a set of counter-arguments: it points out that well-worn notions of masculinity and femininity, by claiming universal and timeless validity, foreclose criticism and possibility of change. Therefore, it would be more effective and useful to locate gender in the history of civilizations and learn to see it as a set of arrangements that evolved at certain points in time. This chapter examines a few important historical theories of gender.

The list of theories described in Chapter 5 is neither exhaustive nor random. I have chosen arguments from political and critical traditions that have elicited active debates within women's movements in India and in parts of Europe, UK and America. I am aware that much more has been said on the subject, but in this book I needed to focus on a certain relevant body of work. Thus there are texts that do not figure here, and even if they do, they are treated generally briefly. An annotated bibliography has been provided for those who would like to read more on the subject. Chapter 6 returns to the everyday world and looks at how gender is embodied, experienced and lived—it is about the making of gendered social bodies.

There are several themes in this book, and each requires a book in itself. I have tried to keep my arguments and descriptions close to the subject of my study: gender, its implications, history and construction. But wherever appropriate I have also examined the manner in which gender identities mesh with, are transformed by other identities—such as those constituted by caste, class, religion, sexual preferences.

In writing this book I have aimed to unpack the idea of gender and present it as a way of viewing the world and the relationships it contains, as an understanding of the workings of power and authority. The book hopes to enable the reader to undertake a fresh and curious analysis of situations we have come to consider normal and given. I have written this book as a feminist, as one concerned with a politics of struggle and transformation—of human subjectivities and intimacies, social and economic structures, familial and social relations. I am aware that there are as many feminisms as there are thinking women (and men). I use the term in a restrictive sense—as political and ethical philosophy, that is marvellously contradictory, inconsistent, fiercely radical and utterly committed to a better and saner world.

I wish to thank Maithreyi Krishnaraj for giving me the opportunity to put my thoughts on the subject together, and for being patient as well as firm with me. I am grateful to Gita Wolf and Jayashree Nambiar for teaching me the virtues of clear, incisive communication and for all the hours of good conversation. I thank Rimi Chatterjee and Mandira Sen for their editorial support.

Chennai, Oct 2001 V. GEETHA

Contents

Introduction

The setting: a classroom in a city in moffusil Tamil Nadu. The context: a workshop on understanding gender. The participants: 25 students from several colleges in the city. No one seriously disagrees with the fact that women lead difficult lives, they suffer gross discrimination and injustice, they are entitled to their freedom, they should be granted equal rights and opportunities, encouraged and supported in their campaigns to secure their rights. There are at least six boys in the workshop and they appear as convinced as the girls that women's liberation is an important and urgent matter.

Yet the participants are perplexed. They do not understand the phrase, 'equality between the sexes'.

Men and women are so different from each other, how can women do everything that men do? Can they work at difficult and physically strenuous jobs? Nor can men do what women do so well and naturally, such as looking after a baby. Besides, men and women experience life differently: women are gentle, tolerant, whereas men are authoritative, impatient. Given these differences, how can we expect or even ask that men and women be equal? Then, again, do we want to be equal in every respect? Nature has made us different, and we can't really change that, can we?

The questions come so thick and fast that the workshop coordinator is flustered. Her colleague intervenes and attempts to explain that men and women may be physically different, but this does not mean that they are therefore innately different from each other. It is society which has decided that men and women possess different traits and attributes.

The questions persist. Somebody brings in hormones: men and women possess different hormones, and these make them different, not only physically but also emotionally and intellectually. Female hormones make women emotional and sensitive, while male hormones make men aggressive and competitive. Someone else mentions chromosomes—it all happens during fetal development . . .

The arguments get more and more complicated and no resolution seems to be in sight.

This time, the setting is different. It is a camp for village-level social workers. Again, the participants are from both sexes. The coordinator poses them a question: why does society discriminate against women?

The answers come pat. God has made women different from men. It is clear that women are physically less strong and capable than men. In fact they need men to look after them. Since men have to be protectors and caretakers, it is natural that they exert authority. This leads to men treating women unjustly. Men speak thus. Women express the matter somewhat differently. Women are meant to be mothers. They embody love and sacrifice. Men do not understand, in fact, are jealous of women's essential nobility and therefore try to control them.

We cannot really expect to change all this, can we? It is like wanting to change the way nature works—so run one set of arguments.

Another sort of argument goes like this. Men and women may be different, but they complement each other perfectly. There is really no problem here: men are bold, women are cautious, men are violent, women gentle. Men are suited to work outside the house, women are perfect homemakers.

'Boys Don't Cry'/ 'Girls Don't Get Dirty'/
'Girls Don't Climb Trees'

HOW CAN MEN AND WOMEN BE EQUAL?

We encounter such ideas—of male and female natures and capabilities, male and female roles and responsibilities—in one form or another everywhere, in our homes, at school, in the outside world, in books, television, religion. We are consistently told what is typical feminine behaviour, we are admonished if we do not behave thus. Our brothers are scolded if they do things boys are not supposed to do, such as cry, if they fall down and hurt themselves. Likewise, we are often reminded that our natures and destinies are crucially inter-linked. Little girls who display an adamant streak in their characters are often warned that they cannot afford to behave like this when they marry and go away to their husbands' homes. Boys are encouraged to be brave and adventurous since, after all, they have to go out into the world and earn a living.

As we grow up, ideas of masculinity and femininity become central to the way we think about ourselves. Many of us actively reject interests which we recognize as untypical of our sex: girls do not really fight to play games, or engage in physically strenuous activity. Neither do boys appear eager to learn cooking or interest themselves in the details of housework and care of children. From their adolescent and post-adolescent years upwards, girls seek to look beautiful, appealing, and sometimes cultivate a deliberate passivity. Boys, in turn, court a macho ideal, swagger into an aggressive masculine identity with which they may or may not feel comfortable. Girls practise coyness, while boys express an unbridled sexuality.

As boys and girls emerge into adulthood, their futures appear more or less fixed, both in terms of their work roles and their emotional lives. Girls assume that they have to get married, raise children, cultivate patience and obedience, put the family interest over and above all else, learn to do with less of everything, accept that women have to sometimes sacrifice their wants for the good of the family. Boys are convinced that once they finish schooling or university, as the case might be, they have to find a job. They also tell themselves that they cannot afford to be light-hearted about life, they have to be serious, learn to be responsible and dignified, bold and dynamic, and not emotional or sentimental.

Very few girls dare to ask why their ultimate destiny is linked to the institutions of marriage and motherhood; or why their inner lives should heed the virtues of patience and sacrifice. Similarly, very few boys imagine a life for themselves that is not related to a profession of one kind or another. Neither do they ask themselves why they have to be consistently tough and brave. Even those men and women who are convinced that women need to be educated and economically independent, or who feel that men can and must share housework and parenting, seldom interrogate what is commonly regarded as the destiny of the sexes: that Nature intended women to be mothers and men to be protectors, that a woman's place is the home and a man's the world; that ultimately women are responsible for the kitchen and the children, whereas men are accountable chiefly to their public roles, as wage-earners and heads of families.

Yet all around us, we find men and women doing things which are considered not typical of their sex. Women do perform heavy chores, physically exacting tasks. There are men who take great pleasure in minding children. We know that there are as many angry and impatient women as men, that not all women are timid or retiring. We have also met men who are shy and diffident, anxious and self-deprecatory. We know too that there are people who are physically not of either sex, who seem at ease moving in and out of male and female identities.

NORMS AND EXPECTATIONS

Clearly, our ideas of male and female natures derive less from empirical facts and observations and more from norms and expectations that govern our lives. Even those whose lives and actions run in direct contradiction to these norms accept the latter's salience. Thus a timid man believes he is less of a man while a bold woman imagines that she is less feminine than other women. In other words, experience is often measured against the norm and found to be inadequate and wanting.

What are these norms and who sets them? Who defines social expectations? Why do we take them to heart, live them out?

Norms that set standards of typical and ideal male and female behaviour favour different roles and responsibilities for men and women. These norms usually have to do with patterns of work, modes of feeling and relating, style of clothing, systems of learning and communication and, most significantly, access to resources and power. Norms and expectations exist in almost all societies, to a greater or lesser degree. They are, however, not unchanging. Nor are they consistent and uniform. Certain norms may be found in one historical period and discredited in the next. During the same period they may apply to certain sorts of women and not to certain others. Expectations are defined in different ways in different societies. With the same society there may exist different sorts of expectations.

Let us consider how some well-known feminine and masculine norms work in specific social and historical contexts. In the Indian context, a woman has necessarily to be a good wife and a mother. But does this norm work the same way for middle class, upper caste women and poor dalit women? The latter cannot and do not devote as much time to wifely duties and responsibilities. They spend a lot of their time working outside the house, alongside their men or separately. Child-care and housekeeping amongst the poor are shared responsibilities. Neighbours, younger women and girls often help out with these things. It is not that poor women do not heed the norm of wifehood and motherhood, but clearly they experience it differently. They are neither obsessed nor paranoid about good housekeeping and mothering. Their primary concerns have to do with food security, survival and safety: is there enough food to last the monsoon months? Will the husband survive yet another season of unemployment and drinking? Will they be able to live without fear of displacement or eviction?

The situation is almost the reverse in the households of middle class, upper caste women. Keeping a good home and rearing a child are considered a woman's particular responsibilities. There may be household or even family help, but these are viewed as supplementary. The wife-mother often feels the pressure of performance, of having to live up to standards that are exacting. This often translates into anxiety about cooking, cleaning, pleasing the husband, the children's education, their clothes and so on. Anxiety, in turn breeds guilt that things are not perhaps as perfect as they ought to be and guilt, in turn, makes the norm seem more ideal and less attainable.

Moreover, for either group of women, this norm is not a constant. For example, middle class women have found it easier to balance the claims of wifehood and womanhood with their own concerns at least since the last quarter of the twentieth century. Changing times, especially the expanding numbers of women in paid employment, have re-defined housework: though it continues to be a woman's responsibility, and still a source of frustration and paranoia, it is balanced by work done outside the home, which instils self-respect and confidence. With poor women, a different logic works, should their lives change for the better. With a steady income and a sturdy house, survival is assured. Whether they work outside or not, they now begin to adhere more consistently to the norm of the good wife and mother. They become more attached to the middle class ideal of housekeeping and motherhood. In some instances, they stop working, considering it a slur on the family honour that women should work when men can take care of the family.

The point is that a norm is powerful and influential, not because everyone adheres to it but because it is made to seem universal, though it works well only in certain contexts. In this case, being a good wife and mother, which is a middle class, upper caste ideal, is generalized enough for all women to want to adhere to it. Poor women accept its pertinence, though their lived realities often subvert and contradict the norm. This generalization of a particular ideal happens in extremely interesting ways. It is made to appear a function of one's sex. If you are a woman, you will necessarily want to be a good wife and mother. In other words, a particular historical and sociological identity is displaced onto the female sex as such, and made to appear natural to it.

Such a process of naturalization is even more evident in the case of social expectations. For instance, men are expected to be virile and powerful. But the truth is, in any given situation, at a particular point in time, only some men are powerful and virile. Yet all men expect to feel this way, irrespective of the fact whether they have the means to exhibit their power or display their virility. Consider poor, underprivileged men in rural north India, for example. Often they are employed on big farms run by ruthlessly feudal landlords. They are kept under strict surveillance and control. Their wives and daughters are even more vulnerable than they are: at any time they can be sexually assaulted or raped by the landlord or his cohorts. In this situation of total powerlessness, how can a man expect to feel either power or virility? But men feel the need to prove their manliness, so to speak, and when they do, it is pitiful and tragic, and exercised at the expense of their wives and children. And even when it is not pitiful, it is merely defiant, as when poor youth in a city slum tease girls from well-to-do families. In either instance, a man feels compelled—whether or not he consciously admits it—to be a man, to act as if being so were natural to him, a proof of his state of being.

In whatever form or forms norms and expectations exist, they are propounded in a systematic fashion. That is, they are not random opinions, held by some and ignored by others. Nor are they eccentric ideas which no one takes seriously. They exist as the very stuff of commonsense, informing the way we behave in an everyday sense.

This does not mean that no one is responsible for these ideas of male and female natures, roles, functions, responsibilities and duties; or that they affect everybody in society in exactly the same way (we have seen that this is not the case). Obviously it is useful and profitable for some people to have the world explained in this fashion. Several others take these ideas for granted because they appear self-evident. In other words, norms persist because we choose to abide by them. Our choices are dictated by social rewards and punishments. If the cost of not abiding by a norm is material deprivation, social disapproval or humiliation, very few of us wish to break the norm. Besides, many of us possess neither the resources nor the power to challenge expected patterns of behaviour successfully. Thus, norms are not coercive rules, it is our behaviour and actions which actualize norms, embody and fulfil social roles and expectations.

Those of us who resist being overpowered by norms often have to content ourselves with personal choices that we pursue on our own. In times of great social upheaval, norms and expectations are often challenged, and even altered. However, as soon as order is restored in society, we find older norms re-asserting themselves or coopting whatever transformations may have been effected.

GENDER

Norms and expectations which define male and female natures and behaviour are essential components of and rest on social and economic systems. These systems in turn are informed and shaped by these norms and expectations. But social and economic systems are also influenced by other things, for instance, caste, religion, language. These in turn influence and shape norms of masculinity and femininity. The question arises: are norms and expectations regarding masculine and feminine roles and actions decisive in shaping caste, class, religion, sexual preferences, or do any or all of these determine norms of masculinity and femininity? This is a difficult but important question. It involves unpacking systems and the ideas which govern them and scrutinizing systems for the ideas they create.

Many thinkers, theorists and political leaders have thought long and hard on this question. This question, in fact, has been central to the thought and politics of women's rights' activists and feminists all over the world. Several kinds of arguments have been advanced and argued and yet there is no easy consensus on the matter. One thing, however, appears settled. It is now recognized that by posing this important question about masculinity and femininity, a significant and necessary category of analysis has been formulated—this is what we call gender.

In its most commonplace sense, gender is a grammatical commodity. It exists in most languages and divides up objects into masculine, feminine and neuter. Usually there is no particular reason as to why certain objects are considered feminine or masculine or neuter. Besides each language does this differently. Gender in language is thus a matter of habit and convention—this is how things have been referred to and this is how they ought to be referred to. However, the term 'gender' has other meanings. It has come to be associated with biological sex. Sex is considered a fact—one is born with either male or female genitalia. Gender is considered a social construction—it grants meaning to the fact of sex. Conversely, it could be said that only after specific meanings came to be attached to the sexes, did sex differences become pertinent.

GENDER AS CATEGORY OF ANALYSIS

What does it mean to use gender as a category of analysis? A category of analysis is basically a methodological tool that enables a researcher to identify and isolate certain elements in the reality she wishes to study. Like caste and religion, gender is both a part of the reality we study as well as the lens through which we view that reality. When we examine masculinity and femininity and the systems that are linked to them, we actually study and use gender as a category of both description and analysis. That is, we treat masculinity and femininity as pertinent features of the reality we wish to study—this is gender as a category of description. But we also try to link gender to other aspects of reality, and ask how, for instance, class and caste are determined and influenced by gender; likewise we ask how class and caste influence gender divisions. When we do this, we use gender as a category of analysis.

In this book we will look at the various meanings of gender and how they work in a given social and historical context. Chapters 1, 2, 3 and 4 consider gender as ideology—they look at various commonplace interpretations of masculinity and femininity. Chapter 5 examines gender as history—as a phenomenon which emerged at a certain time in the history of our species, and which has been interpreted in several different ways.

1

God Made You Different, Nature Made Us Different

Over the centuries, sexual difference has been interpreted variously. Since men and women possess different genitalia, it was assumed that they are different in all other respects as well. Though as species beings, men and women share a great deal, this fact has not been viewed as pertinent.

Interpretations of sexual difference are complex and varied. For our purposes we may classify them into three sets. Each of these three sets of ideas posits a different relationship between the sex of the human body and human attributes, the body and capabilities and finally between the body and human destiny.

The first set of ideas contain arguments which fundamentally derive from religious and metaphysical assumptions regarding male and female bodies and virtues. These ideas have proved to be extremely powerful and attractive and inform even non-religious—scientific and political—views of humanity. The second set of ideas comprise definitions which categorically accept that the two sexes possess innate qualities. These definitions do not really explain why and how innate qualities exist and are more concerned with the implications of masculine and feminine attributes for society as a whole. The third set of ideas offers sociological explanations for the persistence of notions of masculinity and femininity.

RELIGIOUS EXPLANATIONS

The first group of ideas comprise religious definitions and interpretations which claim that men and women have innate attributes that cannot be changed. These inhere in the very bodies of men and women; are, in fact, expressions of the sexual difference between them. That is, genital and physical differences between men and women imply that they possess different qualities. Often, such definitions are traced back to the sayings of a God or Gods, and justified by pointed references to religious texts and customs. Almost all such observations declare women's bodies to be inherently inferior and sinful, and fit to be controlled by men. Or alternatively they claim men's bodies and souls to be the measure of humanity. That is, man is the norm, the rule. Woman is a derivation, and as such is included in man. Men are granted the power to define, interpret, judge and represent the world on their own terms, while women are to be defined, interpreted, judged and represented by men.

On What Basis Do Religions Declare Women to Be Inferior?

Certain Hindu scriptural texts claim that at the very dawn of creation, women emerged as sinful creatures, fire, snakes and poison all rolled into one. The original Manu, author of the Dharmashastra, argues that at the moment of creation itself, women were allotted the habits of lying, sitting around, with an indiscriminate love for ornaments, and qualities such as anger, meanness, treachery and bad conduct. Manu further notes:

> Knowing their disposition, which the Lord of creatures laid on them at creation (ie, their reproductive power, their sexuality, their essential nature), every man should most strenuously exert himself to guard them.

The ancient Greeks who worshipped both Gods and

Goddesses were convinced that men were the measure of perfection, while women were fundamentally imperfect. The philosopher Aristotle holds that women are naturally lacking in intelligence and rationality. Their bodies lack the necessary warmth that make for human intelligence. Being natural fools, women do not deserve to be citizens who could participate in public affairs. They are to leave these matters to their men who could represent their interests better.

Buddhist texts argue that woman's innate nature is bad. A *Jataka* tale states that women as a sex are unable to distinguish truth from falsehood and lies from truth. They are unstable as the sand, cruel as the snake. Another *Jataka* text holds that women are wrathful, slanderous ingrates, sowers of strife and dissension. Their passions are insatiable, for they act according to their inborn nature. Thus the very nature of women demands that they be controlled and disciplined by men.

Christianity maintains that God created man first, and woman next (from man's rib, in fact), and therefore, man is the exemplary human, whereas woman is a secondary and dependent being. The English poet John Milton writes eloquently that God created Man in his image, 'He for God only', while Woman was created as an afterthought, from Adam's rib. Not being in God's image, woman was to realize 'God in him', that is, Man.

Islam too believes that men were created to rule over and manage the lives and affairs of women. 'Men are in charge of women in so far as God has made the one excel over the other and in so far as they spend of their property.' Like Hinduism, Islam also associates women's bodies with impurity. Going to the toilet, on a journey, being sick and touching women are all considered equally impure acts. Those who have done any of these things are enjoined not to pray until they have washed themselves clean.

On the other hand, and for all their devaluing of women, most of these world religions appear reverential and in awe of women's ability to sustain life in their wombs. Either they possess a tradition of Mother Goddess worship, or they celebrate the virginal woman, whose purity lies in the awesome power she is able to exert over her body. Hindu Mother Goddesses are not only legion but powerful and wrathful. Amongst Hindus, the mother is a model woman, self-sacrificing, heroic and essentially noble. There are also traditions of virgin worship amongst certain rural communities in India. The Christian faith resonates with the piety and power of Mary, the eternal virgin as well as the mother of God. The Greeks worshipped Ceres, the Goddess of Fertility, as well as the virginal and wise Athena. For all its horror of the female body, Buddhism values and celebrates the so-called feminine and maternal qualities of compassion and nurture. It also holds in reverence the state of renunciation and chastity and welcomes nuns into its fold. Islam does not deem woman worthy of worship, but very early in its history, it recognized the potency of those cults which did so and lost no time in declaring these heretical and sinful.

How do we interpret these glaring contradictions? For one, religious explanations of masculinity and femininity are historical in nature, though they claim to be transcendent and universal. They evolved over a period of time and contain several layers of meaning. Though all religions claim that women are inferior to men, they feel the need to state and explain this 'fact' at great length. Why? Very early on in human history, human beings appeared to have been awed and perplexed by the phenomenon of birth. Birth seemed miraculous and it looked like only a woman knew what caused it. But once men learnt to domesticate animals, they realized that they too played a significant role in procreation. By this time they had also established themselves as the superior sex (we will see how and why later). They were therefore eager to explain motherhood and birth in a way which did not concede too much power to women.

They came up with an ingenious explanation: women are inferior because their bodies are 'unclean'. They menstruate and give birth, acts which have to do with blood and flesh. Yet they are mothers and as carriers of life have to be respected and, if need be, venerated. Ancient Hebrew texts also suggest that as agriculture became a settled way of life, men began to assert that their 'seed' or semen was the source of the child's soul, and the woman was merely the substrate or field in which it was sown. In this way they were able to deny much of women's power over birth.

Worshipping women as mothers, while devaluing them in every other sense, thus became a way of displacing as well as managing fears about female power and sexuality. Valuing their 'essential' nurturing qualities of love and compassion, as most scriptures do, confirmed the idea that women were naturally and fundamentally meant to be mothers. It is clear that religion prescribes, justifies as well as contains, in an imaginative way, our notions of the ideally masculine and the ideally feminine. It allows us to reverse the equation provisionally but does not enable a questioning of it. Thus we may take comfort from the fact that women are considered loving and compassionate. Yet it does not help us find out why these qualities should be associated with a particular female role alone, that is, with motherhood; or why the possession of these attributes should automatically disqualify women from laying claims to others, such as strength and ambition, which, conventionally, are described as male. Religious texts are paradoxical in another sense as well: they grant men authority in the world and declare their innate fitness to be priests, yet insist that such men heed and worship the feminine principle.

The power and appeal of religious ideas regarding masculinity and femininity are immense. They have survived various transformations in history and continue to haunt us to this day. Neither modern nor democratic political ideas, nor the objectivity of modern science which actively questions the authority of religion, have been able to dislodge completely these ancient notions of the ideal male and female. Indeed, as we shall see, philosophic and scientific ideas are often expressed in and through a language of sexual difference, but now we find that arguments are clinched through an appeal to nature rather than to the Gods. Yet for those who argued thus Nature was as omnipotent as Gods were in earlier times.

IN THE EYES OF SCIENCE

Since the eighteenth century, modern Western science has established itself as a body of knowledge that is rational, objective and supported by verifiable proofs. But in matters of masculinity and femininity, this science has been neither objective nor rational. Take medicine, for example. Medical science from the time of the Greeks onwards assumed that the naturally perfect human body was the male body. The Greek physician Galen (of the second century CE) believed that female sex organs represented an imperfect and retarded state of human development. That is, women were imperfect and flawed versions of men. Galen recounted stories of women spontaneously transforming themselves into men, but said he did not know of any story which narrated a man turning into a woman. He also stated this was not possible, for everything in nature strives towards perfection, and men cannot revert to being imperfect.

As the centuries marched on, medical science in Europe developed in different ways. In the eighteenth century, on account of the new ideas of rationality and revolution, it was not easy to maintain that women were lesser versions of men. At this juncture, academic studies of medicine came up with a new definition: male and female bodies were radically and naturally different. Medieval doctors had said similar things, but they did not hold these differences to be pertinent except for the purpose of reproduction. For medieval people, sexual difference was willed by God and produced by Nature. It did not matter to them how sex and character were linked. God had done his best and the result was there for everybody to see. Eighteenth-century physicians did not wish to concede everything to God and Nature. They wanted to explain the world on the basis of observable evidence and sound reasoning. They argued that male-female differences were not merely genital, but in fact extended to every fibre of their being. Thus each body possessed and nurtured its own distinctive destiny: intellectual and physical strength for men, and motherhood for women.

This link between sex and destiny remained (and still remains in some circles) a virtual article of medical and scientific faith. The authority of science is such that it is often invoked by those who are not scientists themselves to bolster their arguments. In nineteenth-century England, woman's nature as explained and established by science, became a reason to refuse them modern education. It was argued that too much intellectual work would actually shrivel up a woman's ovaries and render her both unfeminine and irrelevant.

In the twentieth century too scientists debated and researched on sexual difference. For instance, some scientists argue that our respective sex hormones cause us, as men and women, to behave differently. Others have tried to study distinctive character attributes, such as aggression and anger in men, in an attempt to link character traits to sex-specific hormones. However, none of these studies have proved conclusive. For one, the sample of persons surveyed or tested for differences is often extremely small, so that one cannot really extrapolate from such a limited sample to the whole of humanity. Secondly, studies of so-called male attributes such as aggression and anger have yielded no significant results. There are as many aggressive women as men. Thirdly, scientists have not been able to prove successfully that hormones influence people's behaviour and attitudes, any more than their family, faith, social mores, history and so on do. In fact, one pair of scientists was forced to conclude that as far as men and women were concerned, hormonal differences did not mater as much as the differences in the way they were raised.

Yet the question of sexual difference continues to haunt science. Even feminists who wish to understand, rather than accept, the arguments for innate male and female characteristics, find themselves trapped by what they originally wished to interrogate. Consider feminist biologists and their understanding of human reproduction. Conventional biology—an area of study dominated by male scientists until recently—views the sperm as the active factor in causing pregnancy. But once women started researching and writing on these matters, they saw an equally and sometimes more aggressive role for the female egg. Their close studies of the egg's activity convinced them that the egg had been denied its rightful significance. But as one feminist points out, these explanations of the egg's behaviour do not really question stereotypes. Instead, the egg is now described in terms which had previously applied only to the sperm. In other words, the equation still stood, only the answers are arrived at through different means.

The point is science is as susceptible to the influence of ideas of masculinity and femininity as any other system of knowledge, though it constantly attempts to distinguish itself from all other knowledges, on the basis of its logic and objectivity. In this sense scientific language too is marked by history—of what people have thought and said over centuries. As long as the language in which we speak, communicate and think has these built-in, historical assumptions regarding male-female differences, the metaphors and similes we employ to explain the world around us are bound to reproduce these differences—even if we are doing science.

IN THESE DEMOCRATIC TIMES

In modern history, the masculine-feminine equation has undergone subtle transformations. From the eighteenth century the authority of religion was challenged by new radical philosophies and new ways of looking at the world. The world was seen not merely as a creation of God, but one in which men could make and unmake laws and values. The implication was that human beings could and must change this world which had gone wrong.

The one event which convinced people that the world could indeed be changed was the French Revolution of 1789. The revolutionaries declared that all human beings were equal and free. This meant that no human being had the right to consider another human being his inferior or slave. All human beings were linked by fraternal bonds.

These ideas—of liberty, equality and fraternity—inspired several women to demand their rights and freedom. If all human beings were equal, then surely men and women were equal. If women had been considered inferior, this was not because Nature made them that way. Mary Wollstonecraft argued that if women appeared stupid and passive, this was not because of some innate lack of intelligence but because women had not been told to cultivate their minds.

> Women are told from their infancy and taught by the examples of their mothers that little knowledge of human weakness, justly termed cunning, softness of temper, outward obedience and a scrupulous attention to do a puerile kind of propriety will obtain for them the protection of man, and should they be beautiful, everything else is needless, for at least twenty years of their lives.

Olympe de Gouges, a French playwright, issued a declaration of the rights of women in Paris, soon after the

French revolutionaries released their declaration of the rights of man. The declaration of the rights of man did not question male superiority and instead defined the father's right over his wife and child as a natural right. Olympe de Gouges pointed out that such a right had nothing to do with Nature and everything to do with men. It was men who had given themselves the right to exert authority over women, and had often used brute force in the exercise of this right. Nature on the other hand, argued de Gouges, had created men and women to exist in harmonious cooperation and had not granted either sex a natural advantage over the other.

Women like Wollstonecraft and de Gouges, however, were not taken seriously. Many men were willing to accept that all human beings were equal, since they all possessed what other creatures did not possess—the faculty of reason. But they were not quite sure if women were as rational as men. Women were not created to be reasoning creatures, for Nature meant them to be nurturing, caring mothers. Jean Jacques Rousseau, the foremost philosopher of the French Revolution, outlined an entire theory of education based on these ideas, according to which boys and girls were to be educated differently, keeping in mind their different temperaments.

Just as several world religions interpreted bodily differences between men and women to assert female imperfection and male control over women, so did these intelligent and revolutionary men of the eighteenth century utilize the idea of sexual difference to deny women equal rights. Rights were thus defined in exclusively male terms. Or to put it differently, women were denied these rights because, being sexually and naturally different from men, and therefore unequal, they did not deserve these rights.

One further example will help illustrate how pervasive was this idea of innate male and female qualities. In 1849, when a French woman, Jeanne Deroin, announced that she wished to contest elections to the

French parliament, several men ridiculed her. One man, Pierre Joseph Proudhon, tried to disqualify her candidacy by arguing that a female legislator made as much sense as a male wet nurse! To which Jeanne Deroin retorted saying that she would agree with his description but then he must tell her which part of his male body was required for the function of a legislator! Though women like Jeanne Deroin attempted to question the meanings attached to sexual difference, such attitudes did not go away and persist to this day.

In colonial India in the late nineteenth century, male social reformers who actively questioned tradition and custom demurred when it came to re-examining notions of masculinity and femininity. Many of these men were engaged in worthwhile activities such as campaigns for widow remarriage and the education of girls. But very few of them were willing to grant women equal rights as men. They were as convinced as their forefathers that women's nature and talents required them, and, in fact, were best served if they stayed at home, looked after the house and raised children.

For example, those who argued that women must be educated also maintained that such an education should not interfere with their innate and god-given qualities. As one reformer argued, women needed to be educated so that they could continue to function in an atmosphere created by the laws of Manu, which had inculcated values such as chastity, love, industry and care of home in them. Others insisted that education must help cultivate women's innate modesty and not instil in them a desire or ambition to step into either high courts or legislative councils. By definition these were male preserves.

The idea is that whatever women do or are urged to do, which is different from what Nature or God ostensibly meant them to do, they must be on guard. They cannot and must not risk doing or saying anything which suggests they are unfeminine. For to be unfeminine is also to be unnatural. As far as men are concerned, they are rebuked if they do not live up to their essential qualities of virility and courage. In other words, men are asked proudly to express and celebrate their masculine virtues, not merely to be mindful of them. During the colonial period, men like Swami Vivekananda exhorted Indian youth to live up to the manliness of their ancient culture. Vivekananda argued that colonial rule had made Indians effeminate—note how a less manly man is akin to a woman, that is, man is always already the norm—and they had to re-learn their masculine virtues. Exhortations to men to be manly prove extremely enabling, whereas cautionary remarks to women to exercise restraint and live up to their essential womanhood are profoundly inhibiting.

From the examples just given, it is clear that men have been able to interpret significant historical changes and developments on their own terms, and to their advantage. So much so, it appears that this is in the very nature of things, that men are active and dynamic. Invariably, and expectedly, such an engagement is denied to women on the grounds that they are inherently incapable of taking advantage of historical changes. Or such changes are viewed as compromising their innate qualities. Finally, history is interpreted in the light of biology!

Take even contemporary media messages to women. They grudgingly accept that the world is a changed place, and women are increasingly visible in positions of power and responsibility. Yet, time and again, we are told—through the worn-out clichés of film scripts—that a woman may be a district collector, a police officer, a scientist, but she cannot afford to forget that she is essentially and fundamentally a mother. Advertisements are as retrograde as films in this respect. Images of working women are used to reinforce what is seen as their primary vocation—they must look beautiful, earn an income and yet be nurturing and home-loving. The ideal woman is one who works at home, at her profession, and yet finds time to keep a good house, attend to her husband and children's needs, all of which she manages without appearing ruffled or tired.

Media images of men are different. Unlike women who have to work hard to remember and act on their innate sense of vocation, men are more relaxed and very much at home in a changing world: travelling, handling sophisticated machines, making decisions. They are even shown in an uncharacteristic new role, which they take to with winning charm: they emerge as caring and thoughtful good fathers. But this does not compromise their essential manhood. Everything a man does, even if it is not conventionally considered a masculine activity, adds to his power and prestige, or as a well-known advertisement byline goes, he becomes a 'complete man'.

2

The War of the Sexes

If men and women are inherently different from each other, as religion and religion-inspired secular ideas claim, what is one to do? Concede that Nature (or God) made man more powerful than woman, or that women are naturally kinder than men? For centuries, in different societies, these ideas have been the stuff of commonsense. They have found their way into poetry and epic, laws and philosophy. One important effect of these ideas has been the emergence of the notion of categorical differences. That is, once you agree that men and women are and will always be different, you are left with two rigid categories of behaviour, thought action, ethics, religion. Masculine and feminine categories are then so taken for granted that you do not demur when people say 'boys will be boys', 'after all she is a girl, how else could she have reacted'. More seriously, such a categorization assumes that all men and all women are similar across societies and will remain so for all time to come.

So pervasive is this idea of two primary divisions of human beings, the male and the female, that categorization pursues a person from birth. In several parts of India, people try to find out what sex their child is, before birth, and if it is the unwanted female sex, they kill it. Categorization exists thereafter at every stage of the baby's life, should it live: feeding is discriminatory, boy babies are nursed for longer periods of time than girls. Clothes are distinctive and draw attention to sexual difference. Girls' clothes are not merely functional. They are defined as important in covering up 'shame'. Children's behaviour also turns out to be very different. Boys are boisterous, adventurous, girls find it difficult to be so, burdened as they are with domestic work from a very early age.

In all these instances, it is not the sex of the child that decides whether it is valuable. Sex is constructed into an idea, the fact of having a penis is granted pertinence. Thus it is not biology which is destiny. What we make of biology, what we do to our anatomy gives meaning to the fact of sex. This granting of meaning to bodies happens in several different ways: clothes, make-up, sports, sexual habits, sex-specific work—a range of things mark and grant value to sex. As Simone de Beauvoir said, we are not born but become women (and men).

In the Western world, the idea of categorical differences has had interesting implications. It has led men and women to assume that boys and girls are inherently suited for some things and not for some others. It has been argued that girls as a whole are psychologically inclined towards the study of the humanities, whereas boys favour science and mathematics. In a book that went on to become famous, Carol Gilligan, an American educational psychologist, asserted that girls are more for cooperation in the classroom while boys are comfortable with competition.

Let us look a little closely at the 'girls like humanities' and boys are good at science' argument. Throughout recorded history, girls were denied access to scientific learning. Science academies and societies in Europe explicitly forbade female membership. Besides, male scientists were asked to keep away from the distracting influence of women so that they could devote their minds to the pursuit of scientific truth. Not only were women thought of as having lesser minds, but they were also considered potentially disruptive of scientific enquiry. Girls could study science at home if they wished to, and some did, with the encouragement of kind fathers or brothers, but they were invariably exceptions. Besides, as the historian Gerda Lerner points out, to do science, one must possess the time, leisure and an enabling, unfettered space to indulge in abstract thought. For women this has been difficult, since the conditions of their lives do not allow them to get away from the distractions of the everyday: from cooking, feeding, cleaning, caring. Caught and enmeshed as they are in detail, how can they think in general and in abstract terms?

Given this history, it is not surprising that girls did not seek out the rarefied domains of scientific knowledge. Studying languages or history at home, learning music or writing verse of fiction did not demand an intensive engagement with institutions and academies of learning, nor did they require long hours of absorbed concentration. The study of the 'humanities' could be pursed in those delicious interstices of time which women found between chores. However, this does not mean that the scientific vocation did not attract women. There were women who tried to teach themselves and actually succeeded in working on their own. But many of them had to endure an enormous amount of emotional privation, loneliness and frustration that it seemed to them that they were perhaps unfit for the job!

Let us likewise consider the notion of cooperation: household economics and management require high levels of planning and adjustment. From a very early age, women learn to balance tempers and moods, to adjust and let go their own desires in order to maintain family peace. They actively cultivate a state of mind which enables them to put other peoples' interests, husbands, children, the old, above their own. This is not to say that all women accept their condition or perform their roles with ease. While some women adjust, compromise and practice self-effacement, as many women are ill-tempered, cantankerous and discontented with their lot. But since most women simply have no choice but to keep the household in order, they became grudging cooperators.

Clearly, and as the feminist historian Joan Scott has pointed out, women seek out those roles and functions for which their everyday life prepares them. We may add that women grudgingly accept these roles and functions by default; they find it difficult to sustain themselves in so-called non-feminine spheres and often end up valorizing their own. But none of these is a reason to argue that women seek out these roles simply because they are women.

WOMEN AS SUPERIOR

Significantly enough, in both Indian and European history, the feminine category has been invoked to assert and justify women's moral superiority over men. Such an assertion fulfils different purposes at different times. Mahatma Gandhi, for instance, eulogized the quintessential different traits of rectitude, self-sacrifice and modesty and proclaimed that women were therefore ethically more evolved than men. Further, argued Gandhi, the Indian independence struggle against the British demanded a critical feminine response. To him women were ideal and natural satyagrahis, inherently suited to carry out his war for truth. In nineteenth-century Britain too, women's characteristic virtues—patience, forbearance and goodness—were hailed as qualities that would redeem the most hardened and selfish heart. Such women, it was pointed out, could reform and lead the most vile of criminals from darkness to light.

In our own times, the idea of women's moral superiority has acquired a sharper edge. Some feminists maintain that compared to men a woman is naturally more evolved and has a greater capacity and vocation for nurturing civilized values. A few feminists have gone so far as to say that men are incapable of nurturing values such as peace and care, whereas women simply will not opt for a violent resolution of conflicting interests. Such arguments have found great favour with social action groups such as those concerned with the environment. Some of these groups insist that women are naturally inclined to be better guardians of the earth; since they give birth, they will not countenance destruction.

Ironically enough of these ideas have helped many environmental movements succeed. In most parts of the world that are poor, women are in charge of getting water, finding fodder for animals and gathering fuel. They have direct experience of the fact of dwindling resources and know only too well the need for their conservation. Therefore they find it easy to accept the arguments of those who say that women are ecologically more sensitive and must participate in the struggle for preserving the environment.

Ideas and action, thus, reinforce each other, though in this case, they have caused no immediate harm, except restating old platitudes, but to different effects. But we may well imagine the situation, were it the other way around. Since men considered women innately incapable of reason, they denied them education. Not being able to read and reflect, women were doomed to ignorance. This then became the reason for denying them education, and so women continued to remain ignorant and men continued to devalue them. In this case, ideas and action matched each other perfectly. This circular logic remained unbroken until women struggled for a life of the mind and began to think and argue matters for themselves. The point is once we act on the basis of categories we assume to be true, then our actions help to keep these categories alive. Change happens only when we prise apart these ways of thinking and begin to re-state and re-form concepts.

MUTUALLY EXCLUSIVE WORLDS

If categorical thought is carried to its logical conclusion, the sexes become two worlds that are mutually exclusive. And then we have no option but to agree that since women and men are so dissimilar and possess perfectly opposite qualities, there are only two options available: either men and women have to learn to see themselves as a complementary pair; or they have to accept that a war of the sexes is inevitable. The idea of complementarity is a very old one—it has been used to justify women's role as housekeeper and mother and affirm men's role in the world outside the home. The notion of complementarity exists in contemporary commonsense as well and is often used to counter and discredit arguments for women's equal rights.

The idea of the war of the sexes is also old, as we find from the world's oldest mythologies. In today's world this idea has a different resonance. Some feminists say all men are aggressive and desire to possess, control and subdue women. Therefore women must be eternally vigilant and seek to build a world that is free of and independent of men. Others criticize these ideas and describe them as perpetuating 'biological essentialism'. That is, we are not saying anything new. From very early on, men have maintained that biologically speaking, women are weak, emotional and in need of male control and protection. We have now merely reversed the argument and claim that men are inherently dominating and brutish. This does not enable us to question the system of values which designates particular qualities to men and women and assigns different and hierarchical values to these qualities. Instead, it allows us to exult in our separate natures.

The dogma of categorizing the feminine has proved enormously attractive. But it is clear that it emerges with particular force in certain historical moments. From the late 1990s onwards, a period that inaugurated unabashed consumerism—in the wake of the globalization of India's economy—several contemporary women's magazines have begun to offer an updated and fashionable version of the so-called inherently feminine qualities. Since women are both economic actors and consumers in today's economy, they have to be appealed to, yet this is not to be at the expense of convention. Advertisers and journalists have come up with ingenious solutions to make women feel comfortable in their new found productive worth, as well as in their socially secondary status. One magazine, for example, proclaims, punning on the title of a popular book: 'Men may be from Mars, but women are just down to earth.' Women's pragmatic housekeeping skills come in for praise, and at the same time, men's roles are dismissed (but not questioned) as irrelevant. Men may consider themselves aggressive, competitive and successful, but meanwhile look at women. See how much they actually do and achieve.

There is another sort of celebration of feminine virtue which also is a product of categoricalist thought. This is the idea that women, as such, will be better than men if only they are educated and given more political power. Variations of this theme were heard loudly during the debates in India on the reservation of seats in Parliament for women. Several women's groups asserted that once elected to office, women will be less corrupt, more considerate towards their voters, and more accountable to them than men have been.

3

Role Play

The third set of arguments accepts that men and women may be innately different, but does not grant that this fact is particularly pertinent. Masculine and feminine modes of behaviour are relevant in as far as they reflect social expectations. Men and women enact different roles, because society expects them to act in these ways and rewards them if they do, punishes them if they do not.

Why do these expectations exist in the first place? Role theory has little to offer by way of a convincing answer, in fact, it accepts different roles as a given, a point of departure. It only allows for the possibility that roles and expectations can be transformed, provided one knows how this system works.

WHAT HAPPENS WITH CHILDREN?

How are social expectations expressed and enforced? Through a variety of practices and institutions. A child acquires its earliest knowledge of its destined role in the family. Parents dress their boy and girl children in different ways. They buy them different toys and books. They have different codes of behaviour for boys and girls. Boys must not cry, girls must never be seen without underwear. Boys can run, jump, climb trees, girls are asked to be careful. In countries like India, there are further distinctions: girls in poor families get to eat less food than boys. They are less likely to be sent to school, less favoured when it comes to buying new clothes or toys. By the time a child is six or seven years old, it has a fairly coherent sense of its sexual identity and the expectations which are attached to it.

Children accept and abide by these roles for two major reasons: they are scolded, reprimanded or punished if they do not. Or worse, they are shamed if they dare to be different. Girl children, especially, learn at a very early age that they will be laughed at, teased, if, for example, they do not wear clothes which they are expected to wear. Often they are teased by their own peers. Boys are likewise mocked at for being 'sissies' should they wish to play with girls.

Schools reinforce some of these expectations: in many Indian schools, for example, girls and boys are made to sit separately, are not encouraged to talk or play together. Segregated classrooms send out signals to children that boys and girls are inescapably, dangerously different. Primary school textbooks are replete with references to distinctive male and female roles. Boy-girl interactions in school are not spontaneous. They are mediated by notions of shame, modesty and fear, for girls, and aggression and awkwardness for boys. An advertisement for a biscuit, popular in the late 1990s in India expresses this perfectly. A schoolboy tears open a packet of biscuits. A girl associates the sound of tearing with a slit hem in her school uniform and embarrassedly pulls her pinafore down. The boy laughs indulgently and holds out the biscuit packet to her, the girl realizes she has been deliberately fooled, and coyly accepts a biscuit.

As children grow up, they find out that everything around them communicates fairly identical messages about growing up male or female. Many things seem to suggest that it is natural and inevitable for men and women to pursue different paths and seek particular and exclusive destinies. These come from the media or from the things parents and teachers say, the books they read, the behaviour of men and women as they conduct themselves at home, on the streets, at work. These norms of masculinity and femininity, for in effect that is what they are, are not merely descriptive. They also prescribe and demand certain sorts of behaviour from men and women. If such behaviour is not forthcoming, punishment is swift. Think of what happened to a female social worker, Bhanwari Devi of Rajasthan. Unlike most women from her state, she dared to do public work. She also attempted something more. She actively campaigned against the practice of child marriage in her area of work. For being forward and daring, a group of upper caste men raped her: as if to remind her that she was after all a woman and must never presume to act out of character. If she did, this is what would befall her.

CHALLENGING STEREOTYPES

Given the force of social expectations, and the fact that they are justified on the grounds of biology, can they be challenged at all? Those who insist that it is society which is responsible for assigning particular roles to men and women argue that this is indeed possible. For example, the content of media messages can be changed. Women can be shown in more enabling and empowering roles. Textbooks can be re-written in such a way that we present men and women as being not really all that different. Likewise male and female roles and functions can also be shown to be reversible. Most important, men can and must be told that norms of masculinity limit them, can in fact prove quite oppressive. The government can be persuaded to reserve a certain number of posts for women in all its departments, including legislative bodies. All these are of course possible and must be done. But will such measure undermine the belief, the idea, that there exist distinctive male and female roles?

We know from history that these roles have

been reversed, if need be. There have been men like St. Francis of Assisi, and in our time, Mahatma Gandhi, who exhibited great compassion and care. Gandhi confessed to feeling like a woman and a mother on several occasions. Heroic female warriors are legion. Joan of Arc and Lakshmibai of Jhansi come to mind. There are also female guerrilla fighters in many resistance movements. Then again there have been power-renouncing kings who retired to the forest to write, and there have been women who ruled for several decades. Today there is no domain of work or achievement which men can claim to be theirs and theirs only. Whatever was conventionally deemed the province of men has been encroached upon by women. Women may not be accepted in their new roles but this has not stopped them from doing what they can and wish to do.

The fact, however, is that whether from the leisure classes or the working classes, women take on male roles, they do this either because they need to survive or because they do not see their sex as a disqualification and simply go ahead to do things, or at least struggle to do them. It is also significant that men have not taken to female roles and functions, as women have taken to theirs. Women's work does not bring prestige or power. Besides there has really been no bar on men doing women's work—in fact, in those instances where men have taken on characteristically female roles and tasks, such as cooking, they have transformed them into professions which fetch money and prestige.

We also need to differentiate here between different classes of men. In countries like India, working class and lower caste men have always helped around the house and obligingly carried and looked after infants. For them, as with their women who work outside the home, such a sharing of work is a crucial aspect of a distinctive culture of survival.

The problem is while to an extent male and female roles and functions have become interchangeable, they continue to *remain* female and male roles and functions. A caring father is like a mother. A working class or lower caste man who takes on female roles is as conscious of roles and identities as any other man. While he may work around the house, he is under no illusion that it is a woman's job. He does it because the women in his house too work. In fact, as working class and lower caste families improve their lives, women stop going to work. They retire into domesticity.

At the other end of the spectrum, successful female professionals rarely view their success as legitimately female. Often they imagine they have 'usurped' a man's place and therefore must do justice to the position that is theirs. Many of them consider it a matter of pride that they are seen as being as tough and efficient as men. Consequently, they learn to eschew their so-called feminine qualities of compassion and gentleness. Significantly Indira Gandhi was often referred to by the Indian press as 'the only man in the cabinet' and there is no record of her having repudiated such a statement.

DO ROLES FIT?

There is a further problem. Assigned social roles also produce and perpetrate emotions and ways of relating that justify these roles. Being a man also means that one is rational, always in control, unemotional and consistently strong. Being female requires that she is patient, understanding, emotionally expressive and compassionate. Roles and emotions do not always exist in a perfect fit—there are irritable and impatient mothers, timid and self-effacing men who are uneasy in their professions. Yet both men and women strive to be as typical as possible, convinced that these are their natural modes of being, often suppressing or downplaying contrary emotions. The irritable mother ends up feeling enormously guilty for not being sufficiently gentle and patient, while the timid man cultivates a huge sense of inferiority for not being man enough.

'ONE OF THE GUYS'

Women who persist in being tough and hard come up against very real limits. They find that they are often unable to find suitable professional positions, though they may be brave and sexually confident, the rules which govern behaviour are such that their courage is often mistaken for brazenness, their honesty for promiscuity. Most important, the world is so arranged that such women find that at best the fact of their sex is ignored and they are treated as 'one of the guys', at worst, they are punished for being different—made fun of, ostracized, physically hurt.

'A COMPLETE MAN'

Men who seek to downplay their given, masculine roles and feelings and be like women, more expressive and emotional, find out—like the 'complete man' who is portrayed in a textile advertisement—that they do not really have to stop being male. They continue to occupy positions of power, prestige and authority. They may spend more time with their children, attending to the old, even lead a rich emotional life, but these emotional transformations do not alter the structures they inhabit. Unlike women for whom a life of the emotions went hand in hand with a limited engagement with the world, less pay, lack of mobility, overwork and loneliness, for men who seek to step out of their ordained emotional lives, there are no such limits.

This does not mean that one cannot afford to be really untypical, or that women somehow are forced to confirm, while men get to have the best of both worlds. This is neither true nor indeed possible, given the ingenuity of human behaviour and action. But the point is social roles and functions exist as parts of real structures of power, of inclusion and exclusion, approval and disapproval, privilege and punishment. These structures are not external to our lives, but are embedded in the ways we work, live, behave and think. Thus protest and resistance need to be continuous, reflected in actual choices women and men make, both in relation to how they wish to live and think and what they wish to do, by way of a living.

4

Masculinity and Femininity: Ideas Are Real

Before we go on to discuss gender as history, we should perhaps pause and reflect on what we have discussed so far. Ideas of masculine and feminine virtues are not fiction. They are real, they exist in the world we live in and affect our lives in very fundamental ways: the clothes we wear, the food we eat, sexual relationships, our very thoughts. They help us make sense of our experiences, understand and formulate our views on ourselves and others in particular ways. These ideas affect men and women differently. Yet these ideas are not static imperatives which human beings receive passively—they struggle with them, re-work them, subvert some, discard others—in every instance the idea becomes real, becomes an aspect of practice in specific contexts.

Secondly, masculine and feminine identities are not the only socially pertinent categories in any society. There are other identities which are important and relevant, and which are as subject to restrictive norms and expectations. Religious strictures, for instance, are as discriminatory against certain kinds of men, as they are with respect to women. For example, in India, only brahmins can claim and perform legitimate priestly functions. Likewise, categorical thought recognizes and defines other sorts of innate characteristics besides masculinity and femininity—it divides human beings on the basis of skin colour and temperament. Thus in racially divided societies, black people are imagined to be innately crude and primitive. Every society possesses a range of social roles and functions, besides those ascribed to men and women. In India, certain castes are fixed into certain functions—scavenging, washing and so on. They are also expected to perform certain roles, for instance, be official mourners, drum-beaters at funerals. People belonging to these castes fulfil the duties assigned to them, for not only is this linked to their survival, but also others, especially higher castes, consider it their vocation and punish them if they do not carry out their prescribed tasks.

It is important to see how gender and other differences intersect and criss-cross in a given social context. Let me explain these two notions with reference to the three sets of ideas I have outlined.

RELIGION AS PROCESS

Most world religions enable men to attain positions of authority in religious matters. Such men alone are deemed capable of interpreting scriptural texts and laying down rules which other men and all women are to follow. Religious definitions and explanations of sexual difference are often used to justify every kind of discrimination and cruelty against women, including practices such as enforced widowhood, sati, witch-burning. Very few women are allowed to read and interpret scripture on their own. But in most religious cultures, women are under greater pressure than men to observe customs and practise rituals and suffer greater punishment, if they do not. When men turn religious zealots, they exhibit their zealotry by forcing women to follow religious strictures in the strictest imaginable way. This may mean observing fasts, wearing a veil, and so on.

But religion does not empower all men equally. It is important to keep in mind that discrimination sanctioned by religion is also directed against powerless men or groups of men such as slaves, or in the Indian context, the shudras and the so-called untouchables or dalits. In fact the *Manusmriti* lumps together animals, shudras and women and considers all of them equally unclean, polluting and fit to be subdued and controlled by the men of the upper castes. Other world religions, Islam and Christianity, for example, do not consign an entire group of men to the low status they reserve for women, unless these men are non-believers, or considered sexually deviant. Homosexuals, for instance, have been castigated as unnatural and sinful.

It is clear that women and certain groups of men are both subject to restrictions and deliberately dis-empowered, at the behest of powerful men, who control access, among other things, to culturally significant experiences and resources, such as those to do with religion. But neither women, nor men, simply receive and accept these restrictions—they react to them, respond in specific ways and, in doing so, alter and transform them.

RELIGIOUS CHANGE

In medieval south India, owing to complex historical reasons, several men from the lower castes and a few women understood religion as an existential personal experience of faith. They overlooked and in some cases eschewed the mediations of brahmin priests, responded to the spirit of religious texts, rather than to their formal significance, defied restrictive social taboos of caste, and, most important, yoked a deeply felt devotionalism to notions of liberation. Significantly, women bhaktins transgressed given gender roles and identities—Akkamadevi, a Kannada poet, chose to discard her clothes, grew her hair long, thus deliberately flouting gender norms which require women to be clothed and modest, and sexually contained. Nudity and long hair, in this case, represented a certain disregarding of norms, which Akkamadevi clearly felt to be irrelevant to her existence in a world of faith. Similarly, lower caste devotees transformed their humble status into marks of spiritual fervour—they cast away felt notions of lowness and claimed, as Chokamela and Nandan did, the heavens for themselves.

It must be pointed out here that religions themselves get altered as they seek to root themselves in specific historic contexts. In the process their strictures with regard to gender and morality produce contradictory and, sometimes, unintended effects. Consider the role of Christianity in the Indian context. It came here to proselytize, convinced of the rightness of imperial British rule. But devoted missionaries of faith were anguished by the horrors perpetrated by caste. They felt that the ideology of caste contradicted the spirit and message contained in the gospel. Thus, missionaries took to educating dalits and other lower castes. In doing so, Christianity, with its schools, hospitals and notions of a common brotherhood in Christ granted to dalits and other despised castes a measure of self-worth. Women who converted to Christianity had access to learning. Besides, they were also inspired by the Christian notion of good work. That is, they could aspire to be of service to suffering humanity, be teachers, nurses. Christianity enabled them experience a sense of vocation that took them beyond their designated roles as wives and mothers.

CHALLENGING THE BIASES OF SCIENCE

I argued earlier that the language of science was not particularly critical or objective when it came to the question of sexual difference. As a result, we have scientific notions of male and female beings which more or less reproduce arguments that assert that women are unequal to men. This has lead to the sciences remaining essentially male domains, and scientific thought refuses to concede that its own conclusions often rely on unexamined notions of masculinity and femininity. Even those women who pursue science seriously have to work within a system that refuses to acknowledge both the facts of sexual difference, as well the meanings that we have attached to them. Science establishments demand a degree of concentration and absorption which women cannot bring to their vocation, should they be pregnant or lactating mothers. While maternity leave is granted to women, many demur from accepting long maternity leave and some are known to fill in these hours of rest, writing and researching papers! Women scientists find they have to function in a context where unless they work twice as hard as men, and prove themselves three times as good as them, they are likely to be discouraged.

Until recently science has played a role in perpetrating theories of racial superiority and inferiority. For several decades, scientists lent their names and credence to theories which maintained that non-white races are innately irrational and cannot be taught the ways of modern science. Though most of these theories stand discredited today, they exist at the level of commonsense, and are invoked from time to time in the service of things such as intelligence quotient tests or in genetic research. It is surely not accidental that science has remained not only a male domain, but also one dominated by white men.

None of these disadvantages have prevented non-white races and women from engaging in scientific research or theory-making. While the scientific establishment remains a white male preserve for the most part, women—and non-white men—have challenged the theoretical assumptions of science in different ways: historians and philosophers of science from non-white contexts have argued that science is as much a product of culture as anything else and that Western science reflects the biases of Western culture. They have pleaded for a more inclusive and catholic view of science, and one that accommodates different notions of truth, objectivity and verifiability than those specified in science as most of us know it.

A NEW POLITICS

The idea that women are unequal to men and therefore cannot be granted citizenship rights continues to dominate political thought and action. Today, unlike in the days of the French Revolution, women have been granted equal citizenship and legal rights in most countries. Yet in many of these countries, women are not at all adequately represented in political parties, legislatures or the courts of law. Even if women are admitted into the higher levels of government, they are entrusted with responsibilities which may be characterized as 'feminine'. They are put in charge of social welfare, mother and child-care, family planning.

The few women who find their way into positions of greater authority do so because they have the support of powerful male politicians—usually father, husbands, brothers. They are often viewed as wives (or widows), daughters or sisters of eminent leaders and not really as political persons in their own right. Political leaders, legislators, lawyers and others in the public realm continue to think and act, as if women's sexual difference implies that they are subordinate and unequal to men. Modern democracy does not demand that a woman be active in the public realm or that she exercise her rights as a citizen. Most democratic institutions are of a public kind and do not really affect or even attempt to influence domestic and familial life. When they do, it is in the form of laws, which, again, are interpreted through a haze of ideas that have to do with masculinity and femininity.

In societies like India and the United States of America which have divided people on the lines of caste and race respectively, lower caste and black men—like women—may be legally equal to all others. Yet only in political formations which are solely devoted to their good, do we find large numbers of these men in prominent or in leadership positions. In so-called mainstream parties, they are almost always consigned to a minority or considered a special interest group. In India, for example, every major political party has a women's cell, a minority cell and a dalit forum—as if these identities cannot be brought into the central agenda of parties and must be necessarily treated as 'special cases'. That is, neither women nor dalits, or, for that matter, minorities can claim a representative, public status—in other words, in themselves they do not constitute a legitimate public and become part of one, only when a political party designates them a particular space and identity.

Clearly, democracy has defined itself in fairly restrictive terms: it allows for formal equality but obviously this is not enough. The mere granting of rights does not help to alter people's attitudes and perceptions regarding those they consider inferior, whether these are women, black people or dalits. But the notion of rights has served women and others who do not possess a public voice and identity to demand that their points of view be heard. In India, for example, the guarantee of formal equality has encouraged dalits and women from claiming equal rights in several ordinary instances. Dalits have demanded rights of equal access to public spaces, have fought against discrimination which follows them, because they are considered 'untouchable'.

Women's encounter with equality has been equally dynamic. The idea that they are equal to men has led them to demand that they be considered as a significant constituency when politicians and bureaucrats make plans—whether this has to do with the budget, or the census or elections. That is, women do not want to be seen as appendages of or as dependent on their husbands. They are becoming increasingly aware that the work they do at home, on the family plot of land, constitute productive labour. This is just one instance of how perceptions can alter once a new idea finds its place.

In recent years, Indian women have been able to experience a sense of the public, feel themselves an active part of it, because of the constitutional amendments which reserves 33 percent of seats in local government for them. Every panchayat today has a significant number of women—while it is true that many of them are timid, mere alibis for their husbands or brothers, the fact that their presence is required in a panchayat, that they possess the power to decide on village concerns, have enabled the more articulate women actually to participate in the democratic process. It is possible that women's sense of themselves, their roles and functions may undergo a gradual transformation over the next decade or so, should the system of local government continue to function.

LIMITS OF CATEGORIZATION

Categorical thinking about men and women is commonplace and part of our everyday lives. Its effects are to be found in many things around us. Spaces are sharply divided into masculine and feminine: the space of home is identified with women, and the outside world is considered an exclusively male sphere. It does not matter that women too engage with the outside world, as workers, consumers, citizens; or that men are active in the family and home, as fathers, husbands, decision-makers. Women's identity rests on their roles as wives, mothers, as home-makers, whereas male identity is linked to productive work, public visibility and power.

This division of spaces reflects the division of work or labour. Women's work at home, whether for the family or at a task that fetches her money, is not considered work at all. It is instead seen as an extension of her duties as a wife and a mother. By definition, the household space cannot be a site for productive activity. The logic of feminine and masculine spaces works in other insidious ways as well. Most women who work outside their homes are confined to those work sectors such as the export garment and electronics trades. Here low wages are the order of the day. It is assumed that women's work is supplementary to the family's income, for after all, her real duty is performed at home and anything else she does is gratuitous. Men's wages alone represent a living wage and their work is 'real' work; primary and necessary.

A significant number of men, especially from the poorer and more deprived classes, are as subject to low-wages work as women and, like them, are often disallowed from protesting for better wages, but they are likely to be more mobile than women. They also are more likely to learn new skills or upgrade existing ones. More men than women work in the organized trades or the services sector, subject to wage revisions and where the learning and upgrading of skills are important.

Though a certain sort of feminism and environmentalism have utilized categorical thinking to the advantage of women, throughout history, this mode of thinking has worked to keep women away from male preserves: higher education, economically empowering jobs, political visibility and power, intellectual life, art. It has effectively confined women to the cramped spaces of the home, to low-paying jobs, denied their mobility, curtailed their desire to go about the world, meet new people, experience life in all its detail. On the other hand, men have derived a great deal of advantage from the simple and seemingly irrefutable logic of categorization. Being male is a condition that exudes power and confers privilege, even if not all men are powerful or endowed with resources to affirm their claims of masculine prowess. Masculinity is, of course, interpreted differently by different groups of men, and to very different purposes. Yet it is seldom dissociated from expressions, enactments and practices of power.

What about racial or caste categorization? Are they as much part of our commonsense as ideas of gender? And do they operate in the same way? Until a century ago, in India, caste divided people up in such a way that they occupied different social and living spaces and remained well within the social roles and work assigned to them. Different castes performed different occupations, and these occupations were arranged in a hierarchy, a system of what Dr. Ambedkar referred to as 'graded inequality'. Each caste was thought to be of a certain temperament, as if qualities were embedded within the bodies of people born into a certain caste. There even existed different legal systems for different castes—brahmins and shudras, for instance, were not bound by the same laws.

Race and caste categorization, however, have received challenges throughout the twentieth century. The doctrine of equal rights as well as the struggles waged by dalits and blacks have helped unpack all those assumptions which constitute categorical thought. The epistemological guarantees which once underwrote expressions of categorization no longer exist, or if they do, they are perceived as prejudicial. Categorical thought with respect to men and women continues to endure, though, as we have seen, it has its transformative aspects—when feminine characteristics of empathy and tolerance are invoked during anti-war protests. But these moments of transformation and subversion run the danger of confirming categorization and do not really produce those attitude changes some feminists hope for.

Categorical thought with respect to gender remains active even in contexts that have actively confronted other sorts of categorization. For instance, anti-race and anti-caste activism have not always recognized the pertinence of gender equality and justice. Dalit men or black men do have a stake in maintaining that as men they deserve privileges and power which women are not to expect for themselves—these demands may not be articulated directly, but they exist in the way men view themselves and women, and in the manner women play out the roles which are defined as theirs. Thus a dalit woman who prefers to remain silent about sexual harassment in the community may defer her anger, because she knows 'boys are like that, and anyway, they are our boys'. Her maternal role and identity come into play here, though in a transfigured manner. A dalit youth who is angry and sorrows over the rape of dalit women may experience anguish, pain, hurt, but often this is at the behest of an emotion that demands that he, as a *father* or a *brother*, avenge or at least mourn, as he should, the dishonour visited on his daughter or sister.

INCOMPLETE SOCIALIZATION

Social pressures and expectations—the role play expected of men and women—have contributed to a hardening of sexual difference. Social expectations—peer pressure, media messages, work options—are subtle and persuasive, as well as direct and forceful. Each of us learns to feel at home in our destined role through negotiation and struggle, and thus confirm its validity. Such negotiations and struggles are different for men and women. For men, the rewards of conformity are: money, status, prestige and celebration of being male. For women, the rewards are less tangible. They gain the love of children, older people, feel virtuous in being nurturing and compassionate.

But in concrete terms women practise a great deal of denial: whether it is food, leisure time, questions of health or sexual desire. Women learn to put them by and attend to tasks that await them as wives, sisters, daughters and mothers. In many cases, women are forced into abdicating desire and want. Or, more particularly, forced into subsuming their needs in the needs of their husbands. Domestic violence plays a huge role in keeping women submissive.

Social norms that are imposed on, say, dalits in India are of a different kind. They are clearly experienced as impositions, their unjust nature is transparent. They are not explained in functional terms and are usually justified on the basis of religious arguments. The play of power in sustaining these norms is all too evident.

Socialization, or the imposition of social roles, though, is never as consistent and seamless as it may appear. In the course of our negotiations with given norms, we are invariably inventive. If, for instance, women are expected to be beautiful in a certain way, there are individual women who bend the rules and push the expected ideal to its very limits. They either flaunt it in a way that makes them alluring and threatening at the same time; or else they make their own rules which do not alter the idea that women are to be beautiful, but which certainly beg the question, what is beauty. Dalits in modern India wear the marks of their low status proudly—they announce their caste identities boldly, claim a long and gracious lineage for themselves, write out caste histories which glorify what is usually reviled.

SUMMING UP

The societies we live in expect us, as men and women, to live, think and act in certain specified ways. But human beings do not merely react to strictures, they also respond, invent and subvert rules. The question is whether such struggles and negotiations with a set of given norms help to confirm and perpetrate these norms, grant them a permanence, or whether human action actually helps to unmake and explode norms. The answers to this question, of course, depend on the way we live, the times we live in and our relationship with others, without whose support or opposition, as the case may be, our actions and thoughts remain private.

At the same time, we must recognize that there are real, material stakes involved in keeping alive and active norms of sexual and other differences. These stakes also extend to linking these various differences—the sexual and the social, the cultural, the economic and so on. Clearly, sexual differences exist in the context of other social differences, even as they impinge on and influence these latter. Likewise other social differences are expressed in and through sexual differences. Thus, in the case of Hinduism, a shudra is like a woman—a case of caste identity being feminized in a derogatory sense. Similarly, a shudra, much like a brahmin and upper caste women, is only fit to serve brahmins and others, and as with women, in such service lies his salvation. In Hinduism, both untouchables and women are polluting—a menstruating woman is literally an untouchable for the days that her period last. Gender and class differences are likewise mutually linked, as we shall see in the following chapter.

What grants masculinity power not only over women but also over other men as well? Why and for what purpose is the fact of being born with a particular set of genital organs granted significance? In what follows, I propose to examine the basis for sexual difference—through the reading of key historical texts which attempt to explain how and through what means men gained ascendancy over women. These texts help us see how sexual difference rests on systems of living and working which we have built over a period of time. Needless to say, such systems not only made men more powerful than women, but also some men came to dominate all other men and women.

5

Gender as History

Historical explanations of masculinity and femininity are diverse. Yet they are informed by a crucial epistemological and political principle: masculinity and femininity are not aspects of biology or physiology. Neither are they god-given. Instead they are parts of systems of thought and action which human beings have constructed over centuries. This means that their meanings and significance are myriad, dependent on time and place, influenced by facts of both geography and history.

Here we will consider four major theories of masculinity and femininity. Unlike other explanations, which we have discussed in the earlier chapters, these are not expository in nature. They do not comment on existing truth, whether this truth is expressed by religion, science or politics, or proclaimed as normative and pragmatic. These explanations of masculinity and femininity are concerned with questions of how, why and when did men and women come to be viewed as essentially different beings.

FRIEDRICH ENGELS: THE WORLD-HISTORIC DEFEAT OF THE FEMALE SEX

One of the most well-known and exhaustively discussed historical theories of masculinity and femininity is the Marxist theory of gender. This theory has several variants and emphases, but its fundamental hypothesis is clear and coherent: gender is not an isolated piece of reality, it has to be seen in relation to the social whole, to what Marxists refer to as totality. That is, ideas of masculinity and femininity are neither normative, as religious doctrine would have us believe, nor do they exist as categorical imperatives. Male and female roles and functions are not just functional—they do not merely reflect social expectations. They exist as aspects of a social and economic system. In this sense, they reflect, express as well as influence social and economic realities: of economic power, social dominance and cultural authority.

Marxism as a system of thought emerged in the nineteenth century, when capitalism as an economic system was becoming dominant. Marxism set itself against the exploitative nature of capitalism, objecting to and challenging capitalism's exploitation of thousands of workers, whose labour was utilized to build huge profits. Meanwhile the workers suffered a truncation of their creative faculties, were underpaid, and made to work in terrible conditions. Marxism analysed society with the intent of liberating the workers from an oppressive capitalism. It sought to understand the oppression of workers in order to persuade people to act to change that reality.

In order to understand Marxist formulations on gender, we need to know the concepts used by Marxists to understand reality. Before we begin, one thing needs to be made clear. Marxist theories are reflexive: they constantly seek to question their own premises, because Marxism believes that understanding is a dynamic process. In other words, one engages with the world in order to not only understand it in itself but also to see if that world can be transformed into a better one.

One of the more important arguments of Marxism is this: human beings make their own lives and they do this through two interlinked material processes: production and reproduction. Production comprises all those tasks and activities performed by members of a society to secure their basic needs: food, shelter and clothing. Reproduction refers to the specific task of bringing children into this world and raising them to adjust to and accept the world they grow up in.

Production and reproduction are crucially linked because to be able to grow food, or build a house, one needs to survive. Survival needs an enabling context—where one eats, sleeps, is looked after when old or sick, where one finds companionship and love. The sphere of reproduction, the family, efficiently organizes daily living to this end and thereby enables production to go on. Marxism postulates that every society organizes production in specific ways. Thus the production of food, shelter and clothing in any society follows a certain pattern or mode, depending on what is being produced, how it is produced and who produces it. The mode of production is not static. It changes over time.

Modes of reproduction are both physiological and cultural: women give birth and thus literally produce children who go on to occupy their appointed roles in the production process. A landlord's son inherits his father's lands, a washerman's son inherits his father's profession. But women play another major role in the mode of production. They sustain relationships, family unity, raise children, and socialize them into accepting their roles in the production process. They do this in many different ways. One of the most effective forms of socialization happens through culture and religion. Often women are the bearers of culture and faith, they actually take charge of most family rituals and observe religious codes faithfully.

There is another concept linked to production and reproduction; relations of production and reproduction. Production is not merely a matter of work and how one does it. Every act of production, be it hunting, fishing, farming or building requires two things: the actual technical means through which things get done; and the human labour which makes this possible. This labour is never free or independent, except when one is working on one's own piece of land or running a small shop. Often labour is hired or enslaved. In olden days, labourers were procured through abduction and slavery—in wars between early human communities, the losers were enslaved by the victors.

Later on, human societies everywhere came to comprise two distinct groups: those who owned resources and power, and those who had only their skills and labour to offer. The former exercised control over production, but were never, except in rare cases, direct producers. The latter were the actual producers, the workers who made crops bloom, whose skills produced temples and cathedrals, but they had to work for those who could pay them, employ them and ensure their survival. This relationship between those who labour and produce and those who own resources is a production relationship, that is, essentially one of power. Those who control economic resources exercise power and authority over those who do not possess anything but their labour power.

Relationships of production are organized differently in different societies. In India, for example, caste is an important production relation that determines the work one does, and more important, defines one's access to resources. If one is a dalit, one is immediately marked as untouchable, powerless, fit only for certain tasks. If one is born into a brahmin family, then one assumes that learning and schooling are one's inalienable rights, that these are one's given avocations. If one is a Rajput or a Bhumihar, one is born to land and power.

Relationships of reproduction are somewhat different—they involve individuals, not social groups, such as the rich and the poor. There are emotional ties between individual men and women. Marriage is the most persistent and common form of relationship between the individual man and woman. Marriage and children go to constitute the family as a set of relationships. Relationships of reproduction vary from culture to culture. They are also more resilient and stable than relationships of production—in this sense they may straddle different modes of production.

Relationships of production and reproduction intersect at various points. In caste society, for instance, the marriage relationship in a poor dalit labourer's household is vulnerable to disruption by the landlord who, at any time, can demand sexual access to the labourer's wife. Feudal land relationships and the caste system together mark the lower caste woman's sexuality as 'available'.

Under the same system, an upper caste woman's sexuality is considered precious, something that has to be carefully guarded and protected, from the ostensible and imminent rapacity of lower caste upstart men. In this context, chastity is linked to caste honour, which, in turn, becomes an emblem of power.

Modes of production and reproduction change and give way to newer forms. This happens when the relationship of production, for example, the relationship between a factory owner and the worker, reaches a point of crisis. Many economic and political factors may bring about this crisis, but once it happens, then, neither older production relationships, nor the mode of production which sustains these relationships, can persist as before. A revolutionary situation is created and this becomes the crucible for the emergence of a new mode of production.

Modes of reproduction are more intractable to change. Family forms change slowly and incrementally. Since the family is the site of generational and emotional ties, it possesses an intrinsic tendency towards continuity and conservation, and it constantly attempts to shore up the world of the individual in the face of economic or political revolution.

As I had remarked earlier, in the Marxist view reality is dynamic and systematic. Reality is constantly being made and re-made, as human beings strive to lead their lives within a certain mode of production. A landlord may be cruel and rapacious, but the labourer manages to rebel now and then, a successful factory owner has to contend with militant workers who insist that he share his profits with them. In other words, it is human agency, the actions of individual men and women, on their own, or as a group, which makes reality, even as that reality forces them to act in certain ways. Therefore Marxists hold that history has to be seen as human history, as something created by human beings in their struggles for a better life. They also argue that this history is best understood as a history of class struggle, of contentions between producing classes and the owning classes.

Marxism addresses the question of masculinity and feminity in the context of a theoretical terrain defined by these various concepts, and utilizes them to explain how women became subordinate to men. What is decisive in the making of masculine and feminine norms and expectations? Is it the mode of production or the mode of reproduction?

The Origin of the Family

Friedrich Engels, Karl Marx's comrade and fellow thinker, writes at length on these matters in his famous *The Origin of the Family, Private Property and the State*. He suggests that early human societies were egalitarian. There existed a simple and functional division of labour, 'a pure and simple outgrowth of nature', between men and women. Men hunted, fished, provided the raw material for food and made the tools necessary to carry out these tasks. Women cared for the house, prepared food, clothing and looked after children.

> Each was master in his or her own field of activity: the men in the forest, the women in the house . . . The household was communistic, comprising several and often many families. Whatever was produced and used in common was common property.

The woman was at the centre of the communistic household, for often she alone knew who the father or fathers of her children were. Sexual relationships within the household were freer than we know them now. Women could choose their men. They, in fact, controlled the household, the men were mere visitors who could be asked to leave when the women did not want them.

Things changed when human communities settled in one place for a long time. Earlier, human beings lead an essentially nomadic existence, wandering from place to place in search of food and water. Once they started living in a stable environment, they learnt to grow crops and began to raise animals. Now food ceased to be a day-to-day problem. They could not only meet their everyday food needs, but could also store and use surplus food. As human beings produced more food, learnt to make and use tools, and began to practise animal husbandry, they had a range of goods at their disposal. Once the production of these goods accelerated, the communistic nature of society changed. Fights between groups became common, as they fought over resources. Often the victors carried away the losers to work as slaves for them. This created what Engels called the 'first great division of society into two classes': masters and slaves, the exploiters and the exploited.

Gradually as groups accumulated wealth, the relationship between men and women changed, for all the wealth was a result of production, essentially a male activity. Domestic work and the household, where women had wielded authority over men and the group in general, lost its significance.

> In the old communistic household, which embraced numerous couples and their children, the administration of the household entrusted to the women was just as much a public, a social necessary industry as the providing of food by the men.

But when production became more valued than the household,

> The administration of the household lost its public character . . . It became a private service. The wife became the first domestic servant, pushed out of participation in social production (p 73).

Household labour was devalued and women became domestic slaves.

Thus, the division of labour, once a 'pure and simple outgrowth of nature' ceased to be in favour of women. The growing significance of production created a new institution: private property. For men who produced more and more of everything wished to keep all of it for themselves. Private property was not only land, animals or slaves, soon it came to include women as well. Men wanted to own women, so that they could gain control over the children, something which they needed to do, if they had to pass on their wealth to the next generation.

With a woman being deemed a single man's property, her control over her children also loosened. Earlier, children inherited through their mother, rather than their father, which is predominantly the case now. Inheriting through the mother was known as mother-right. But when women lost their exalted status in the household, mother-right too gradually disappeared. Over a period of time, children learnt to identify their descent and inheritance through the father. By this time, the woman and her household had ceased to be central to the group's life. Now, the man and his house and property assumed importance and men became valued group leaders. This is how patriarchy—the rule of the father—came into existence.

Engels characterizes the transformation of women into property and the disappearance of mother-right as the 'world-historical defeat of the female sex'. With women becoming the property of men, sexual love ceased to be free and of advantage to women. A woman was now bound to a single man and gradually, monogamous marriage became the norm. This meant that a woman had to be chaste and loyal to her husband, but he did not have to be likewise. Since he had economic power and sexual authority, he could choose to have several mistresses and wives. Engels argues that as communistic households slowly dissolved under pressure from private property, their internal relationships also deteriorated. Spontaneous sex-love and promiscuity gave way to degrading and oppressive relationships. Therefore enough women welcomed sexual regulation and control, and when monogamy emerged, they actually felt it was an advance on whatever they had known earlier.

In Engels' view, the historic defeat of the female sex and the emergence of patriarchy led to a devaluing of female tasks, roles and responsibilities, and a consequent valorization of male roles and functions. This also led to sexual hypocrisy in marriage and a chauvinist sexual ethic in society. Men wanted wives and families, and at the same time claimed their right to older sexual freedoms, in the form of extramarital relationships. Women on the other hand were enjoined to remain chaste and loyal to the idea of monogamy.

Though Engels does not write at length on the specific features of masculinity and femininity, he is clear that female lives, trapped within the realm of reproduction, were doomed to unfreedom. Engels suggests that for women to reclaim their humanity, they would have to necessarily enter the realm of social production.

> The emancipation of women and their equality with men are impossible and must remain so as long as women are excluded from socially productive work and restricted to housework which is private. The emancipation of women becomes possible only when women are enabled to take part in production on a large, social scale, and when domestic duties require their attention only to a minor degree.

Engels argues that modern industrial production which

requires women's labour as well as men's would prove advantageous to them, since it would give them economic independence and, more important, force a re-organization of the household. In fact, it would generate a demand for the conversion of private domestic work into a public industry. Thus, the family would cease to be a 'private' institution and become truly social. Though Engels is scathingly critical of capitalism as a system of economic slavery, in which rich industrialists lived off the labour of workers, he understands the capitalist system as essentially contradictory. It thrives on exploitation but at the same time creates the social conditions in which this exploitation could be challenged. For women, capitalism is a moral horror since they have to work in terrible conditions and are forced to neglect their homes. Yet work outside the home earns them an income, makes them socially productive. Besides, capitalism has created the means—large-scale social production—by which all work, including housework, could be organized on a public scale, which would benefit women. He brings together two struggles: the workers' struggle against capital and women's struggle against confinement within the devalued sphere of reproduction. Workers are enjoined to take collective possession of large-scale production in the interests of a common good and to secure justice for all, while women are asked to join workers in this struggle, so that they could re-organize production to accommodate mothering, child-care and nurture.

Engles's description of how society works and how male and female identities, roles and functions came to be defined are useful in several respects. Firstly, Engels demonstrates to us that the basis for male dominance is male economic power and sexual authority. Secondly, he shows us how the subjugation of women implies not only a devaluing of her as a person, but of her role in reproduction, that is, as mother and as one who creates the human and familial context for relationships. Thirdly, he suggests that male dominance and female subordination, and by implication masculine and feminine norms and ideals, are the products of history, and therefore subject to change through human effort. Fourthly, he outlines the general historical context when such changes may be effected in the context of industrial growth under capitalism.

ENGELS RE-VISITED

Engels' theory of gender, of the evolution of male economic power and sexual privilege, offers a complex explanation of how women came to be enslaved. Some feminist thinkers, however, have found his premises problematic. Their objections are several. Some object to Engels' hypotheses and arguments, others to his prognosis. For our purpose, we will divide these critics into groups.

The First Group

The first group of critics accepts the theoretical viability of the broad Marxist framework within which Engels operates and agrees that the evolution of masculine and feminine norms have to be seen in the context of material life, of production and reproduction. They also agree that male authority was established as a result of their securing control over production. But they have problems with some of his assumptions.

They point to a basic flaw in his arguments: Engels assumes that there is something like a natural division of labour, which is 'a pure and simple outgrowth of Nature'. This is true only in the most literal sense—that Nature intended women to be mothers. But reproductive labour is more than the physical act of giving birth. It comprises a range of tasks—cooking, cleaning, nurture, education—none of which, except nursing the child, requires the exclusive services of the mother. So it is wrong, they argue, to assume as Engels did, that women fell into reproductive tasks because this was ordained by nature.

Neither is it true that men were or are the sole producers. There is enough evidence to show that women shared production tasks with men, in the past as well as in the present. Likewise, there is evidence from studies of different cultures and societies that reproduction itself is not homogeneous. Every society organizes the business of housework, child-care and nurture differently, involving different sets of people, both across sex and generations. For example, in rural societies in Africa and Asia, children are looked after by neighbours, elderly male relatives, even male youth.

These critics point out that the valuing of social production over and above the household and reproduction cannot be seen as a universal phenomenon, as Engels thinks it to be. Social production, in some contexts, did not exclude the household and instead was based on a vigorous household economy—that is, the household was not merely the site of reproduction, but of production as well. Women laboured both as biological mothers, as cultural teachers and as producers (we see this, for instance, in weaving communities in India, where the loom is often the centre of the household, around which both men, women and children work, with women bearing the additional burdens of securing food and caring for children).

Even where social production happened at a different site, outside the household, and became the basis for exercises of power, it did not always result in the emergence of private property and the monogamous patriarchal family. Communal control over resources, or ownership by rotation on the basis of kinship, was found throughout the ancient world and is present in non-Western cultures to this day. These economies possessed their own correlates: polygamy, extended families, complex kin networks.

The implications of these criticisms are significant: production and reproduction can only be meaningfully discussed in terms of specific social and cultural contexts. Descriptions and interpretations of the evolution of these spheres of human activity offered by Engels are richly suggestive, but they are not universally applicable. That is, they are not iron laws, and are useful only when they are contextualized. Most important, the sexual division of labour which Engels assumes to be natural must be seen as historical: due to various culture-specific reasons, biological reproduction became the sole defining activity of women. However, here too, history proved decisive, for different cultures weighted reproduction differently.

Further, the relationship between production and reproduction needs to be precisely established for different historical and social contexts. That is, one cannot assume that in all contexts, the household was subsumed into the sphere of production in the manner that Engels describes it. The household existed and exists in a dynamic relationship to production, influencing, directing and constituting the production process in specific ways.

The Second Group

The second set of critics finds Engels' arguments about the origins of male power problematic. They argue that it is not men's control over production that made for their dominance. Rather it is their control over reproduction that made men powerful. Basing their arguments on the work of the French anthropologists Claude Levi-Strauss and Claude Meillassoux, these critics of Engels suggest that women first came to be controlled by men through an exchange process between different communities. Women were exchanged as 'gifts', for marriage (in South India, the custom of taking a bride from a family and in return marrying a daughter into that family is still extant), and for ritual purposes.

The exchange of women happened at a time when human society was in a state of transition—from an earlier stage centred around the woman and her household to a later stage when men sought to gain control over women. During this transitional stage, the relationship between men and women came to be regulated. Certain taboos were instituted which forbade sexual relationships, for instance, between brother and sister. These taboos created set patterns of male-female relationships, as a result of which women not only lost free sexual access to men of their choice, but also came to be seen as important objects of exchange. That is, men began to forge relationships with each other through women, demanding women as brides, and offering, in return, their labour to the family from which the bride was to be secured. In some instances, women were 'exchanged' as hostages during fights between different groups of men.

The process of exchange became the basis for women's subordination: firstly, they became objects; secondly, they lost access to their bodies and sexuality, and lastly, they were reduced to their reproductive worth. Gradually, the exchange of women became a norm, leading to specific and important changes in the status of women: marriage entailed that women move into their husbands' homes. Women were thus displaced from their immediate and familiar context. Moreover, childbirth proved alienating since the children were considered the property of the men and could only inherit through them.

There is a variation on this argument: some feminist historians suggest that Engels's idea, that large-scale production of grain and other goods, using slave labour, was instrumental in the subordination of women needs to be re-thought. Rather it was the prior enslavement of women through abduction and sexual violence which created a precedent for other kinds of slavery. After men had invented rape as a way of keeping women under control, it became easy for them to extend that self-same aggression towards other men. Once they secured control over powerless men, they had access to slave labour, which helped them expand the production process and create the institution of private property.

Why did men abduct and rape women in the first place? Fights and skirmishes between early social groups over scarce resources resulted in deaths which often lowered the ratio of men to women in a given group. To compensate for the loss of men's lives, the victors forced women from the other side to live with them and bear children. Alternatively, and for the same reason, a marauding group abducted women and forced them into sexual slavery. In this context, rape became a weapon to force women into child-bearing and to acknowledge and demand male protection. This protection often resulted in a woman being confined to the overlordship of a single man.

Those who address male control over reproduction introduced a new concept: patriarchy, or rule by the father. Patriarchy was seen as a system which existed alongside systems of economic exploitation, organizing male control over female sexuality and the sphere of reproduction. The exchange of women, abduction and rape were viewed as salient aspects of patriarchy, as so many means through which female sexuality was sought to be controlled. This control was exercised in the interests of male power and gradually institutionalized at several levels: work, culture, custom, religion, education.

Patriarchy was thus an old system, pre-dating the coming of private property and the monogamous family—as the arguments just delineated make clear. In fact, argued the theorists of patriarchy, patriarchal attitudes and relationships shaped and formed the institutions of private property and monogamy. Therefore, the liberation of women will not be complete without the destruction of patriarchy. It is not enough if women join workers and overthrow capitalism, they still have to wage a battle against patriarchy.

The Third Group

A third set of critics object to Engels's forecast that the subordination of women will end only when they enter production. Juliet Mitchell's work is important in this context. In one of her early essays, 'Women: The Long Revolution', Mitchell suggests that neither male control over production nor their appropriation of the female experience of reproduction are solely responsible for the exploitation and subordination of women. The social and economic structure that locks production and reproduction together must be seen as comprising four levels, each of which, in distinctive ways, perpetrate male dominance and ensure female submission. This does not mean these levels function completely independently of each other, but each of them affects human lives in specific ways.

JULIET MITCHELL AND THE FOUR LEVELS OF CONTROL

The four levels are: production, reproduction, socialization and sexuality. Mitchell analyses these four levels in the context of contemporary society both in terms of the changes which have taken place and with respect to what may be expected in the future.

The sphere of production has to do with work: not only the sexual division of labour, but the assignment of different sorts of productive work to men and women. Mitchell argues that under capitalism, women work in jobs which are less paying, require less technological expertise and which are largely service tasks—women are mostly secretaries, nurses, receptionists, and so on. Mitchell also points out that the educational system underpins this economic system, for women study courses that equip them for little else but service functions.

Reproduction has to do with child-bearing and rearing. It is usually considered women's work. It is related to production both directly and indirectly. The family itself was a production site in medieval times, besides being the context for raising children and looking after them.

Socialization is a crucial component of the experience of reproduction. It refers to the many ways in which women and the family raise and prepare children to fit in with the demands of the world. The family does not perform its socializing functions in isolation. It exists in a dynamic relationship to the world outside. This includes not only the sphere of production, but also the worlds of religion and culture, of community life and custom. Sexuality is usually subsumed in reproduction, but it has to be viewed as an integral experience over which women have little control and of which they have only a limited and habitual knowledge.

For Mitchell, each of these levels develop in ways that are not always congruent. Production may be technologically advanced, giving rise to complex relationships in the workplace: the growth of trade unions, factory councils, and so on. But this complexity may be entirely absent in the sphere of reproduction. A radical, unionized worker may be a conventional husband and father who merely wants an agreeable wife and mother. His radicalism may not extend to his questioning the familial system which supplies the world of production with a steady stream of workers and which socializes these workers to accept the world as they find it.

Then again, in some societies, the sphere of reproduction may change—not merely due to changes in production, but in response to changes in its own inner logic. For example, when contraceptive technology became widely available in parts of the Western world, more and more women began to opt for voluntary pregnancy. This also helped them dissociate sexual love from marriage and motherhood. However, this freeing of sexuality was not accompanied by other sorts of freedom for women: from housework, for example, or from low-paying jobs. Moreover, it was not always the women who had the final say in how these technologies were used on their bodies. The point is that in any given society each of these levels affects gender relationships and re-defines norms of masculinity and femininity.

> The liberation of women can only be achieved if all structures in which they are integrated are transformed. A modification of any one of them can be offset by a reinforcement of another, so that a mere permutation of the form of exploitation is achieved.

Mitchell points out that socialists, following Engles, had called for women to be inducted into the workforce, assuming this would automatically ensure their liberation. They had, however, nothing to say about how the sphere of reproduction ought to be transformed. Engels himself had merely said that the tasks of the family should be socialized, meaning that they should be undertaken by public institutions. He had indicated that when this happens the family, as we have known it in history, would wither away. Others within the socialist tradition and who pursued his arguments further had nothing more to offer: often they contented themselves with demanding the abolition of the family. What was important in this context was to problematize Engels's prognosis. And this is what Mitchell does. She notes that, yes, women had to be liberated into production, but equally from forced child-bearing, child-rearing and sexually dissatisfying relationships. For only then would human relations in their totality change.

For Juliet Mitchell, the four levels she describes were ultimately parts of a single structure, which, in the final analysis was determined by the male world of production. That is, though each of these four levels have to be understood in themselves, they have to be seen in relation to production. This does not mean that the entry of women into production alone would free them, as Engels imagined, but it does mean that the economic liberation of women is central to her total liberation.

THE CREATION OF PATRIARCHY

One of the most coherent theories of masculinity and femininity has been outlined by Gerda Lerner in *The*

Creation of Patriarchy. Lerner works with Engels's formulations, as well as with the insights provided by the theorists of patriarchy, but subjects them to an original interpretation and refiguring. Most important, she utilizes these refigured arguments to examine evidence from ancient societies. Based on this, she goes on to outline a theory of how women and men came to live under patriarchy.

Lerner's arguments are based on evidence from archaeology and ancient law and archaic art and sculpture from Sumeria, Mesopotamia, Egypt and Assyria. She builds on the idea of women as objects of exchange and goes on to point out that this has to be understood, not as an appropriation and objectification of women, but of women's sexuality and reproductive capacity. That is, though women were abducted, or given away in exchange for male labour, they were not always passive victims who submitted to their fates meekly. Though they were less free than men, women did utilize their positions of power or limited power to act, whether directly or covertly.

Lerner also distinguishes between different sorts of female powerlessness. She notes that the position of women was

> expressed within degrees of unfreedom on a spectrum ranging from the slave woman, whose sexual and reproductive capacity was commodified as she herself was; to the slave-concubine (mistress) whose sexual performance might elevate her own status or that of her children; then to the 'free' wife whose sexual and reproductive services to one man of the upper classes entitled her to property and legal rights.

Gerda Lerner's account of the subordination of women and the institution of masculine control traces the creation of patriarchy through the following stages:

1. Men appropriated women's sexual and reproductive

capacity through a complex process involving abduction and sexual slavery.

2. The exchange and abduction of women created the basis for the control of their offspring as well. The power of older men over women and children and their desire to safeguard their resources for future generations may have provided an important impetus to the coming of private property.
3. Later, as grain agriculture spread and kingdoms came to be established, law and legal strictures were invented to perpetuate the patriarchal family system.
4. As men learnt to exercise control over women, they extended their authority over other vulnerable groups: thus slavery emerged, in tandem with the growth of private property and the spread of large-scale grain cultivation.
5. While men's power was established and expressed through the control they wielded over the mode of production, women could only get what they desired through the sexual ties they had with men.
6. Even though women enjoyed no direct power, they continued to be venerated and worshipped for their creative and fertile powers. Even after they were sexually and economically disadvantaged, women continued to be priests, oracles, shamans.
7. Women could not really transcend their limited situations because men and the patriarchal system systematically excluded them from education and access to different sorts of knowledge.

Lerner suggests that even if women's biological power to bear children worked against them in the past—most women were abducted so that they could be made to bear children to the abductors—there is no reason why this should be considered an absolute and natural vulnerability, valid for all times and places. Perhaps, both men and women, together, decided that women's reproductive role was central to the species' survival.

Women may have consented to be 'pawns' in exchange, unable to foresee what this would mean for them in the long run. However this may be, it is clear that it was human choice and action which determined the outcome of things.

If patriarchy is a historical product, then it can and must be challenged. For one, the societies created by patriarchal thought are highly inegalitarian, repressive and exploitative, both of human beings and the environment. In such societies the experiences and emotions of vast segments of the human race are excluded from civilization, are not recognized as culturally pertinent. In this context, argues Lerner, it is important to bring women back to the stage of history, by making their lives and experiences, their submerged histories relevant and central to civilization.

Gerda Lerner's study has proved influential, for it was one of the first to link historical information with theoretical arguments. Her methods of analysis has inspired other studies which are equally persuasive. For the Indian context, Uma Chakravarti has provided a richly suggestive analysis in her essay 'Theorising Brahminical Patriarchy' which is discussed later in the book. Further, Lerner's observations, regarding women's relationship to power, through the mediation of sexual ties on the one hand and through religion and ritual on the other enables a view of women not as absolute victims. They emerge as complex beings, whose lives are determined by their access to money and resources, their use of sexuality and faith.

BECOMING MEN AND WOMEN: FREUD AND PSYCHOANALYSIS

Psychoanalysis offers one of the most influential and thought-provoking arguments about the making of masculinity and femininity. Though these arguments refer to the making of individual identities, as individuals mature from infancy to adulthood, they possess a historical dimension since the constitution of individual men and women always happens within specific historical and social contexts.

Psychoanalysis is famously associated with the life and work of Sigmund Freud. Freud understands human consciousness as comprising several levels: there exists a conscious level, to do with everyday behaviour, speech, thought and action. But this conscious level possesses an internal dynamism, that is, it responds not merely to outside stimuli, impressions and influences it receives from the world, but also to an internal logic. This Freud terms the logic of the Unconscious. The Unconscious is murky, inchoate and unpredictable—the seat of instincts and drives which human beings are barely aware of. As a human person grows up, these instincts and drives are repressed, but not in a merely negative sense. Instead, they are channelled, regulated, disciplined and forced to observe certain norms and rules.

How does this happen? Here, Freud differentiates between three aspects of the Unconscious: the id, which is the depository of raw drives and instincts: the individual self, or the ego, which is endowed with capacities for thinking, feeling, wanting, anticipating and imagining; and the superego which watches over the ego. Significantly, the superego is not completely alien or external to the ego—it is simply more in touch with and receptive to external norms and regulations. It is in fact 'an accumulation of parental and other didactic injunctions', which it stores and utilizes to guard and guide the ego.

The id, the ego and the superego exist in a tripartite relationship, each impinging on the other to constitute an individual's conscious self. The deeply instinctual id is basic to the functioning of the ego, but unless the id is brought within a measure of control and discipline through the cautious supervision of the superego, the ego cannot be a stable and consistent entity.

Masculinity and Femininity

Freud's theory of human consciousness is central to his understanding of masculinity and femininity. As children grow up, they acquire a sense of themselves, others and the world around them in and through a dynamic process, involving the id, the ego and the superego. For Freud, one of the most important phases in a child's psychological growth—that period when the ego is stabilized—is the time when the child discovers that it is an entity in itself. This happens when the child can actually differentiate its body from that of its nursing mother. This stage is followed by the discovery that it needs to distinguish itself from its bodily functions—most children play with their own urine and shit until they are slapped away from either. Later on, this reprimanding extends to the child playing with its genitals—it is taught to observe 'shame'.

The series of reprimands, of do's and don'ts, inscribe themselves onto the Unconscious as a set of commands which go on to constitute the superego. The superego marshals the instinctual urge to play with shit and genitals in such a way that the child grows up with a sense of itself as separate, with distinctive boundaries. This is the beginning of ego-formation.

Something crucial happens at the stage when little girls realize that their bodies are different, when they find out that they do not have a penis. This is extremely significant, according to Freud, for this urges them onto a different developmental path than boys. For girls, affected by a sense of lack, suffer 'penis envy', and this makes them dislike their mothers, for, after all, it is the mother's fault that daughters are like mothers—they do not have a penis. On the other hand, they long to be with and like their fathers. They want to possess the father's penis and when they realize they cannot, like mother, they want a child from him, as a sort of compensation.

The development of boys is different. For their part, boys realize that they are deeply affected by their mothers, in fact, want to be with them, be linked to them. However, there is the father, who clearly is entitled to be with the mother, in fact, assumes it as his prerogative. The little boy thus envies his father, but also experiences guilt and fear—guilt because he understands his desire as illegitimate, fear because he thinks his father may take away his penis from him. (This is the famous Oedipus Complex—the name is derived from the story of Oedipus Rex, who unwittingly murders his father and marries his mother, and is punished for this sin.) This fear of 'castration', as Freud calls it, propels little boys to seek assertive power, be like their fathers, emulate their position, power and authority.

Freud's argument is: children experience an undifferentiated erotic desire to be with the parent of the opposite sex. When this wish is not granted, or annulled, through taboos and rules, the wish gets transformed. The ego capitulates to the didactic warnings of the superego, which tells it that as a boy it cannot desire its mother, or as a girl hope to have a baby in place of a penis. This is the beginning of the ego's identification with a norm that is given to it, in place of the wish which is not granted: this norm pushes the boy to be like his father, while secretly fearing him, and makes the girl long for a man like her father and a baby.

In Freud's scheme of things, the wishes that are refused do not go away. They are repressed, pushed deep down into the domain of the id, and there they remain, until in adult life they re-emerge, at exactly the time when the young experience love and courtship. The young man now looks for a woman, who will ultimately marry him and mother his children and him, whereas the young woman's desire for a child and a man who can give her a child in return, forcing her, inexorably, as it were, into motherhood and marriage.

Freud thus locates the beginning of masculinity and femininity in a psychic process which he insists is central to all human development. In *Civilisation and Its Discontents,* he provides a historical context for his theories of human development and repression. He now argues that the repressions which operate in a child's life, in the context of the family, assume a greater resonance at the community and social levels—entire systems of action and thought are brought to bear on the repressed wish or desire. Taboos, restrictions, law codes, sexual norms, courtship and marriage systems—in short, the entire realm of culture and custom comes to structure repression. That is, the repressed wish is displaced onto another terrain: though it does not engage with its original object of desire, for instance, the mother in the case of the little boy, the wish looks to fulfil itself in and through the love of another woman. Likewise, other urges—raw, creative energies, that are usually compulsive and brutal—are sublimated in fabulous works of art. In this sense, repression becomes a state that creates alongside of what is repressed, an entire civilizational system. Or, repression and civilizational growth exist as two moments of the same process of instinctual control and regulation.

Freud observes that the process of repression is complex with respect to women: for in place of the forbidden desire of the girl for her father and the boy for his mother, society created a norm to channellize the desire: monogamous marriage, with an emphasis on female chastity and an enabling of male promiscuity. This norm existed in relation to other norms, such as sexual ones. Since girls experience the absence of a penis as a lack, they are sexually doomed; they can only feel incomplete and passive. Boys, however, looking to overcome penis envy, learn to feel themselves powerful and feel empowered by sexual energy. This leads to greater levels of repression in women and render them prone to all sorts of neurosis.

At another level, the institution of marriage leads to a general disciplining of erotic energies; these are to be expressed in and through reproductive or genital sexuality. That is, sexual desire is deemed legitimate, only when it serves the purpose of intercourse. This obsession with genital sexuality leads to a fragmentation of sexual energy; men find compensation for this through a recourse to other sorts of creative activities, whereas women have to content themselves with mothering.

Freud's reading of human development is both particular and abstract—he bases his observations on case studies, but goes on to tease out arguments of a general nature from these. He is aware of the immense complexity of human nature and never meant his suggestive concepts to be more than measures that help one map a particular human situation or condition. In a historical sense, his theories offer us a way of looking at how norms of masculinity and femininity are embedded within individual psyches, even as the forces which define these norms are social. The superego is the voice of society, of institutions whose do's and don'ts the ego seizes on and internalizes. Little girls and boys become recognizable female and male persons, not merely in a psychic sense, but also in a social sense—the girl's desire for a child is also one that society approves of.

WITH FREUD AND AFTER HIM

Jacques Lacan

Freud's theories have been criticized, re-interpreted and subjected to broader and more suggestive interpretations by other psychoanalysts, notably Jacques Lacan. We shall consider these various re-readings of Freud briefly for what they tell us about masculinity and femininity. Jacques Lacan understands the Unconscious, the realm of the inner life, to be structured like language, that is, the ego is born into a linguistic reality, into what Lacan calls the symbolic order. The little boy who fears castration and the little girl who longs for a penis both seek to identify themselves not with a physical organ but what it represents. In most instances, the penis represents an idea, the form of the desire experienced by the girl or the boy, or what Lacan describes as the 'phallus'. The phallus is like the signifier, the form of a word, which distinguishes one word from another. The phallus exists as a pertinent signifier, drawing to itself expressions of desire, serving as the form through which this desire finds expression. Thus the little boy who fears his father, as well as the little girl who longs for a penis, both experience desire in and through the phallus. The phallus is symbolic of the law of the father, argues Lacan, or patriarchy—this law requires the boy and girl to position themselves in distinctive ways in relation to desire.

Lacan's ideas have interesting implications: they suggest that historically the making of masculinity and femininity are subject to specific sorts of patriarchal systems—each of them function like signifiers in language, allowing, enabling, and, by the same token, disciplining the expression of desire and meaning. The French feminist literary critic Julia Kristeva argues that the law of the father represents the stranglehold of social and cultural convention which can only be subverted by the suppressed instinctual energies stored in the Unconscious.

Karen Horney: The 'flight from womanhood'

There exists several pointed critiques of Freud—some of these were advanced from within the theoretical context outlined by Freud; others refused the validity of some of his assumptions. Karen Horney, for instance, argues that women do not necessarily experience 'penis envy'. She notes that little girls are clearly aware of themselves as female—they recognize the existence of both the clitoris and the vagina. They are curious about the penis in little boys, but this cannot be taken to represent envy, nor do they experience a lack. If at all they feel inadequate, this is because they experience a 'flight from womanhood', caused both by their fathers' rejection of their desire to identify with them and the social devaluation of women. Thus, we need to problematize the notion that little girls measure themselves against their brothers; in fact it may be said that boys feel a sense of lack with respect to girls. This, in effect, represents an incipient form of 'womb envy', of the fact that women seem to possess the gift of life.

Simone de Beauvoir and Alfred Adler

Horney's writings of Freud found favour with several generations of feminists. Simone de Beauvoir refers to her work approvingly and agrees with her and other female psychoanalysts that for the little girl her body is quite complete. If at all she feels a lack, it is because, argues de Beauvoir, she finds herself differently situated in the world than the boy. Here, she also draws on the writings on Alfred Adler, another disciple of Freud, who points out that the valorization of the little boy's manhood, as incarnated in the penis, by his parents and their peers, grant it a prestige, which renders the little boy a more important being than the little girl. This infuriates the latter, sometimes fills her with envy. Yet this itself is not determinate. What is central to her sense of herself, observes de Beauvoir, is the fact of her social difference, that she is accorded a different and inferior affection, in comparison with her brother or her male playmate.

Gloria Steinem: Phyllis Envy

More recently, the American feminist Gloria Steinem has provocatively challenged Freud's theoretical assumptions. In a witty and sharply written piece she suggestively and creatively argues that Freud's assumptions are ultimately an expression of routine male prejudices and dogma about women. In this entertaining semi-fictional essay, she creates Phyllis Freud, who discovered womb envy and successfully psychoanalysed 'testyria'. By successfully reversing gender identities and presumptions, Steinem shows how Freud's theoretical edifice makes sense only within a patriarchal world-view.

Dorothy Dinnerstein: Mermaid and Minotaur

Other critics and re-readings of Freud focus on the role of the mother in the making of identities. Dorothy Dinnerstein's interesting and provocative interpretation of Freud is a good instance of this sort of interpretation. In *The Mermaid and the Minotaur*, she takes a close, sensitive look at the experience of mothering, in terms of the child's sense of its nurturing parent, as well as in terms of the power relationships that mothering creates and enables into existence. Unlike Freud, who focused on the child's growing sense of its own sexual identity, Dinnerstein considers the pre-Oedipal stage of a child's life, when it first comes into a consciousness of its separateness from the mother, with whom, until then, it had a symbiotic, unified relationship.

According to Dinnerstein, this stage is fraught with fear, anxiety as well as reckless joy for the infant who longs to be reunited with its mother, to be helpless and protected. Being separate, it is cruelly aware of the mother's role in its life, a provider of food, nurturer, teacher, who commands as well as cajoles, loves as well as punishes. At the same time, the infant rejoices in its separateness, its will, so to speak. This complex welter of emotions, notes Dinnerstein, is very unsettling for the infant, who is tied to and yet longs to escape the embrace of the mother—seeking approval, yet wanting to assert its own individuality. It knows that the mother is its immediate and most important contact with the world outside. Desiring to move beyond her hold, the infant develops a strong sense of defiance, vindictiveness, anger fear.

Dinnerstein argues that the experience of helplessness as well as the desire for autonomy is common to all children. But boys and girls do not respond in a like manner to this experience. As boys become men, they express an arrogance towards anything female. On the other hand, all their actions are calculated to impress, seek the approval of the woman, a throwback to those days of infancy when mother was the one who offered and withheld approval. Girls respond differently. They grow up to disdain and scoff at other women, actively dislike them, or, to paraphrase Dinnerstien, serve themselves up to men, actively collude in men's devaluing of them, in men's control over them. It is as if by doing so they experience a vicarious pleasure, sharing the vengeful anger of men who have never been able to live down the terror and fear of infancy.

Dinnerstein suggests that the historical and social consequences of female mothering can be understood in two ways; firstly, in terms of the maladjusted unhappy adults it produces, and secondly, in terms of how it perpetrates, justifies and sustains a strong sexual division of labour, not only in an economic and social sense, but in an emotional sense. Men, who grow away from their mothers, come to be at home in the world outside, working, fighting, ruling, but at the same time, they lose touch with the world of nurture and care. Women inherit this, and are ineffectual in the world outside. This makes for unrestricted male dominion on the one hand and for female mothering on the other.

For the child, the father exists, says Dinnerstien, as a distant, affectionate figure, who has somehow escaped the mother's complete power and is at ease in the world outside. This makes him attractive and, unlike the overwhelming, suffocating presence of the mother, he appears as part of an ordered, outer world, rational and open. So much so that for adults who have grown up in the shadow of mother, male dominion appears an 'inexorable emotional necessity.' This is how masculinity comes to define and order the world on its own terms, while femininity remains tied to the emotive world of the kitchen and cradle. Dinnerstein views this situation as intolerable and destructive, for it gives men rights to power, and women, the right to love and nurture, each remain locked in their experiences, thus perpetrating the effects of this splitting of emotional energies. If this situation is to be altered, then mothering, and the sexual division of labour that holds it in place, must be transformed. In addition other modes of parenting must be explored and the workplace rearranged to accommodate women.

Carl Jung

Freud's descriptions of the evolution of masculine and feminine identities elicited a major counter-response from his one-time associate and later rival, Carl Gustav Jung. In what follows, we shall briefly consider his ideas. Jung argues that our inner lives—he refers to it as 'psychic life'—cannot be defined solely in terms of sexual energy. This was his major point of departure from Freud. For Freud, as we have seen, the individual consciousness arrives at a sense of itself through a series of sexual conflicts going back to infancy. Jung thought differently: an individual's consciousness as well as her Unconscious carries residues of human history, of human pasts that go back into early civilizational time. Thus the infant's desire for its mother represents, not a tabooed wish, which will be ultimately subordinated to the norms of patriarchy, but an archaic wish to return to the darkness of birth, only to be re-born as an individual creature a sort of psychic baptism that the child needs, if it were to emerge as a person in his or her own right.

Jung further argues that human consciousness carries the impress of what the individual in question represses as unbecoming, animalistic, primitive. He calls this 'the Shadow', within whose range the individual has to live.

But consciousness also possesses an internal image of the opposite sex—the soul image, 'anima' in man, the 'animus' in woman. A man intent on asserting his masculine identity consistently would thus equally relentlessly deny the existence within him, of a female self. Similarly, women banish male desires and fantasies to the shadowy realms of the Unconscious, where they lie dormant, erupting when the stable articulate personality is beset by crisis. Yet the soul image edges its way into the individual consciousness towards a creative resolution of identity, so that the anima or animus is not, perpetually and disruptively, at odds with the normative role an individual assumes for himself or herself.

Jung's ideas derive from certain occult notions of human consciousness—as comprising opposing characteristics. A person's dominant character often subsumes and overwhelms its opposite, though the psychic health of the individual depends on a complex harmony between the two. This harmony is not to be had as if it were a given but negotiated.

Jung's ideas are interesting for what they tell us about the evolution of individual identity. Unlike Freud who saw this in combative terms, Jung views the individual's assumption of a gendered identity as a process that involves two equally valid categories; the male and the female selves are not cast in a dominant-subordinate position here. Instead, it is assumed that the one needs the other for resolving questions regarding one's individual self. The female principle, or character, is not viewed as a lack, a failed man, but as an essential component to the process of our growth into a healthy adulthood.

AGAINST OUR WILL

American feminists who were active and vocal from the 1960s and 1970s produced a rather provocative and powerful description of the making of masculinity and femininity. These theorists shifted the argument away from production and reproduction. They did not ask which of these spheres was more instrumental in securing male domination. Instead, they concentrated on the experience of sexuality. Whether mandated and structured by particular modes of production, or organized around specific relationships of reproduction, sexuality, argued these women, was fundamentally oppressive for women. They argue that sexual ethics and practices cannot be seen as an expression of another and prior domination exercised by the power and authority of, for instance, private property.

Catharine MacKinnon

Catharine MacKinnon, an American feminist thinker and lawyer, argues rather compellingly:

> In my view, sexuality is to feminism what work is to Marxism . . . By saying that . . . I mean that both sexuality and work focus on that which is most one's own, that which most makes one the being the theory addresses (that is, a worker in the case of Marxism and a woman in the case of feminism).

MacKinnon goes on to say,

> As the organized expropriation of the work of some for the use of others defines the class, workers, the organized expropriation of the sexuality of some for the use of others defines the sex, woman.

That is, female-ness and femininity are both the result of a process of forcible theft of woman's sexuality. Deprived of what is hers, she is forced into subordination.

The analogy that she establishes with Marxism, however, does not work all the way. Workers rebel against capitalism, she argues, but women comply and buy into the system that makes them subordinate. They do so by agreeing to be protected wives and grateful lovers. Worse, they accept their secondary status as their rightful due. In such a society, women learn to disvalue and deny their desire to the point that they participate in their own self-destruction. 'Because sexuality arises in relations under male dominance, women are not principal authors of its meanings.' The content of sexuality in fact demands and eroticizes the subordination of women. That is, women learn to experience their powerlessness and devaluation as pleasurable. For men, this powerlessness, on the one hand, and women's collusive acceptance of male sexual authority, on the other, prove enormously empowering and feeds into their sense of themselves as essentially and powerfully virile and dominant.

To overcome this utterly demeaning condition, women need to speak out, against the violence of men which passes off as love, against an eroticism which demeans them. MacKinnon's fervent plea in the cause of female anger and desire was simply this: 'I say, give women equal power in social life. Let what we say matter... Take your foot off our necks, then we will hear in what tongue women speak.'

Susan Brownmiller

Several others too viewed masculinity and femininity as norms that had emerged from within the terrain of sexuality. Susan Brownmiller writes in *Against Our Will: Men, Women and Rape* that men's sexual power over women and the violence with which they sought to exercise it constitute the basis for female subordination. Arguing that throughout history, rape has featured as a mode of controlling women and keeping them in a state of perpetual fear, Brownmiller suggests that rapists are not socially aberrant people but ordinary individuals whose actions express publicly what all men feel and do privately.

That some men rape provides a sufficient threat to keep all women in a constant state of intimidation, forever conscious of the knowledge that the biological tool must be held in awe, for it may turn to weapon with sudden swiftness born of harmful intent.

Andrea Dworkin

Andrea Dworkin, who worked closely with Catharine MacKinnon, brings a different emphasis to discussions of sexuality and sexual identity. In her book *Intercourse* she looks at sexual love in specific contexts and argues that for most married women, violence is the context in which intercourse took place, whereas for men, intercourse is the context in which the conjugal relationship assumed significance. She thus implies that sexual intercourse between men and women is a characteristically violent phenomenon. Dworkin locates her observations in wider social contexts, drawing on historically specific reasons to validate her argument. Yet the burden of her thought appears essentialist, something which is evident, for instance, in her studies of pornography. Pornography, for her, is the most blatant expression of male violence against and contempt for women. Discussing a particularly vicious instance of visual pornography, she argues that the power of sex, in these matters, is ultimately the power of conquest. The woman is the absolute victim, captured, ready to be tortured and abused. Conquest is naturalized, made to seem an essential male thing. This is achieved by likening the woman to an animal. Dworkin goes on to say, 'The power of sex in male terms is also funereal. Death permeates it. The male erotic trinity—sex, violence and death—reigns supreme.'

Adrienne Rich

Adrienne Rich writes on male sexual identity and culture as being indifferent to women, but brings a very different historical and theoretical edge to her arguments. She looks critically at heterosexuality—or the practice of men and women turning to each other for sexual pleasure and gratification—and suggests that it is neither natural nor inevitable. That is, men and women assume they have necessarily to cohabit and have sexual relationships, but this assumption needs to be interrogated. Firstly, sexual strictures with respect to women are so insistently laid down that they beg the questions: What are men afraid of? What do they imagine women would do, if their sexuality were not controlled? Secondly, male power over women—the exploitation of labour, the sexual use of women in marriage and prostitution, the limiting of women's mobility by keeping them tied to the house, the withholding of education and knowledge from them—expresses itself best through strategies which keep women tied and available to men and men alone; which seek to convince women that marriage and a sexual preference for men are their inevitable lot.

Given this curtailing of women's sexuality and their bondage within heterosexual marriage relationships, is it not evident that men fear women would desert them for other women—not only for sexual love, but for every other sort of comradeship? Having posed these questions, Rich goes on to argue that precisely because it is neither natural and all too coercive, heterosexuality must be understood as a norm which imposes a certain kind of femininity on women, along with prescribing a valorous and powerful masculinity for men. This norm not only devalues women in several respects but also actively works to subsume her sexuality which, Rich suggests, may be at home in what she describes as a 'lesbian continuum'.

This continuum comprises a range of female intimacies, and not merely those of a genital, sexual kind. It includes the sharing of rich, inner lives, the bonding against male tyranny, the giving and acceptance of female support and advice, the comradeship of work—the list is endless. A lesbian continuum offers a different experience of sexuality and the self, says Rich. It is not negative, neither man-hating nor choiceless (that is, women look to each other not out of despair but for deep emotional reasons). It is never recognized or accepted by women, but is most certainly there, feeding into our lives. Lesbian love is the most articulate expression of this inner life, and has to be understood as a protest against heterosexuality and all that it implies, both as a system and as a sexual practice.

To Rich, masculinity and femininity are both social ideals developed within the matrix of what she calls compulsory heterosexuality. As such they need to be subjected to acute criticism. Once this matrix is challenged, identities become unstable and are thus malleable and can be re-imagined.

These various descriptions and theories of sexuality and identity postulate a crucial and central role for the experience of sexual love whether as violence, hetero-sexual passion or repressed homosexual love—in expressions of gender. They have been criticized precisely for this reason: firstly, that they suggest a narrow and singular definition of sexuality, and, more important, they use extremely limited and questionable evidence to illustrate their arguments. They extrapolate from literature and specific historical examples to elucidate and criticize contemporary social practices. These criticisms are individually valid—Catharine MacKinnon does appear insistent at times on a singular and undifferentiated conceptualization of sexual experience and sexual love. She does not account for the play of other factors, such as race or class in constructing female identity. Andrea Dworkin does extrapolate from literature, utilizing her reading of specific literary texts to advance huge claims about female and male sexual identities.

Yet these women, and others like them, writing from within a tradition of public action and advocacy, do illuminate for us that murky area of human experience where the body and ideology meet. This is where acts of violence against women are ultimately linked to cherished and closely held notions of the female body, female desire and female usefulness. These notions are present across the social spectrum. Experiences of other forms of powerlessness, such as those imposed by race or class, do modify the details and expressions of these notions.

UNDERSTANDING HISTORY

These various historical explanations of gender have travelled across cultures, they have inspired several historically and culturally specific accounts of gender. These theories have been used partially, combined in extremely imaginative ways, and in the process they have acquired interesting emphases. In what follows we will look at some theories of gender in the Indian context which represent re-worked versions of some of the theories just discussed.

Periyar: Property, Caste and Gender

One of the most sophisticated theories of gender to emerge in the Indian context was that advanced by E. V. Ramasamy Periyar, an anti-caste radical and original thinker who lived and carried out his agitational propaganda in Tamil Nadu. Periyar argues that masculine and feminine norms are not given. There exist only a set of human norms—anger, pride, courage and so on—and as many women as men experience and express these emotions. Even maternal love is not a natural feeling. Periyar argues that except for nursing the child, the infant could be looked after as well by its father as by its mother. Periyar submits accepted notions of femininity to a scathing critique—beauty, chastity and motherhood, he notes were convenient and elaborate fictions which not only convinced women that they were destined to be subordinate and subject to men, but also enabled them to delight in and welcome that subordination.

Likewise, he suggests that masculinity is merely an expression of brute male power. In this sense, it is the greatest obstacle to female freedom. Periyar is particularly critical of sexual standards which excuse, legitimize and even celebrate male promiscuity, while condemning women to either a life of limited monogamy or wretched widowhood. He undertakes an exhaustive critique of chastity and its converse, female promiscuity. Arguing that the chaste wife and the prostitute mirror each other, he suggests that the one connotes lifelong sexual slavery to one man, while the other sells herself to several men. In either case, femininity is condemned to servitude.

What was the basis of masculinity and femininity, both of which were obviously social constructs? Periyar locates the existence of these norms and attributes within a social and economic system which historically had come to favour the male and mandate a law of the father. This system also possessed the sanctity of religion. Thus, economics, masculinity and a spiritual priesthood together held it in place. Periyar's descriptions and critique of this interlocking social system appeared inspired by Engels's work, though he embeds his ideas within the recognizable context of caste Hindu society.

Periyar argues, following Engels, that after man had successfully established his rights to private property, he took woman as a wife into the household. This enabled him both to enlist her services to protect his property and supply him with progeny, and to lay exclusive sexual claims to her person. Chaste wifehood became a norm, and motherhood an ideal and virtue. Valorized for these roles and destinies, women too learnt to value themselves thus, securing thereby their insubordination and an unequal social system, which allowed some to hoard wealth and forced others to work at producing this wealth.

Periyar notes, however, that there is a distinctive and significant dimension to motherhood in caste society: the desire to have children who would inherit one's name and wealth assumes a certain resonance, on account of the religious reasons that are habitually advanced to justify this desire for progeny:

> After it had become the norm for people to want children to safeguard property, brahmins who had invented fictions of heaven and hell to keep the poor from robbing the rich and to amass some of this wealth for themselves now argued . . . man must have a [male] child who would keep alive his name after death and perform his yearly obsequies (*Viduthalai* 11.10.48).

Thus even as the real historical reasons for wanting children—to safeguard property—fades into the recesses of communal memory, the fictitious reasons invented by brahmins came to take hold of the Hindu male imagination. Motherhood came under increasing pressure for now it was deemed significant for the reproduction of an unequal social order in this world, as well as the next!

The inscription of female sexuality within the terms of private property and caste, argues Periyar, was reified by the institution of marriage. Here, Periyar links the servitude suffered by castes low in the social hierarchy and the subordination of women:

> Just as how Brahminism condemns a very large portion of the working population to shudrahood, so it has condemned women to the servitude of marriage . . . To the extent that a woman lives up to the norms of a chaste and ideal wife, to that extent she accepts and revels in her slavery (*Viduthalai* 28.6.73).

Marriage, observes Periyar, regulates and disciplines women's familial and reproductive labour, even as it actively denies their desires and rights to a self-respecting life of their choice. Of whatever caste or class, the bond of marriage, he argues, invariably renders woman a property and slave of her husband.

Like feminists of a later time, Periyar understands that relationships of reproduction, especially the norms, ideas and practices which govern them, are partially instrumental in keeping men powerful just as men's access to productive resources and political authority does. He was convinced that only by wilfully refusing to play their destined roles within the reproductive sphere and making their own intellectual and sexual choices could women actually free themselves from an oppressive social and economic system.

Periyar's critique of gender is not merely descriptive, it also mandates change, in fact it is advanced to persuade women to re-think their attitudes to love, marriage and motherhood. To enable them make their choices with a greater sense of ease, Periyar and his followers advocated reforms in marriage laws, supported women's rights to education and employment.

Understanding Brahminical Patriarchy

A more scholarly founded argument on the interlinked themes of gender, class and caste has been put forth by the noted historian Uma Chakravarty. In a pioneering essay 'Conceptualising Brahminical Patriarchy in Early India', inspired by Gerda Lerner's *The Creation of Patriarchy,* she argues that patriarchy in the Indian context has to be situated in its relationship to other structures and within a historical context. Taking her cue from Lerner's observations regarding modes of control over women's sexuality in societies that were emerging into highly stratified and closed structures, she makes the following arguments:

1. Gender roles and identities emerge from and, in turn, constitute the social context of caste society: 'A marked feature of Hindu society is its legal sanction

for an extreme expression of social stratification in which women and the lower castes have been subjected to humiliating conditions of existence.'

2. Caste society followed earlier and more egalitarian social formations, for instance, hunting-gathering societies, which predated caste society valued women's productive labour and held in awe women's capacity to reproduce.
3. The gradual emergence of a hierarchical caste and property order and its consolidation marked a distinctive shift in social attitudes to women. For now, in these new social formations, not all women were engaged in production. Women belonging to families that were wealthy or owned land found their labour restricted to housework. They were enjoined to be mere mothers. At about the same time, women's sexuality, once evocative of reverence and fear, now came to be viewed as wild energy that must be carefully controlled and husbanded. To enable this process of control and husbandry, women' movements within the social order came to be restricted:

> Women are regarded as gateways—literally points of entrance to the caste system. The lower caste male whose sexuality is a threat to upper caste purity has to be institutionally prevented from having sexual access to women of the higher castes, so women must be carefully guarded.

4. The guarding of women required that their sexuality be channellized into legitimate channels, 'into legitimate motherhood within a tightly controlled structure of reproduction which ensured caste purity (by mating only with prescribed partners) and patrilineal succession (by restricting mating only with one man)'.

5. The control of women was secured through a mixture of coercion and consent—coercion exercised through her husband, the king's laws and the priest's dictums, whereas she consented to be her own moral guard. Her consent was obtained through an elaboration of virtues that she was enjoined to make her own. Chastity was the most prized virtue of all. It was declared to be her given ethic, her dharma, something that she should strive to sustain.
6. Women had to observe their dharma, failing which their essential animality, their wild nature, would take over their lives.

Uma Chakravarty's suggestive essay and her re-working of this argument in her subsequent writings, for instance, in *The Life and Times of Pandita Ramabai,* indicate that femininity in the Indian context may be understood as an ethic that women had to practise. If they do not, they fail to achieve transcendence, they remain locked in their low, given natures. Her work also helps us understand why and how women consent to this ethic. They are persuaded to view themselves as capable of a greater virtue than what their nature allows them.

Prem Chowdhury

There have been other attempts to study the way gender, class, caste and state interlock in the Indian context and create norms : for men and women, rich and poor, upper caste and lower caste. Prem Chowdhury's study of peasant society in Haryana across a century, carefully and with a wealth of detail, unravels relations of production and reproduction, as they exist within an agricultural economy. Her work presents an account of gender where control over women's labour—as well as control over her sexuality—are essential to the existence of a hierarchical peasant society.

Psychoanalysis in India: Sudhir Kakar

Dinnerstein's arguments figure, with very different implications in the work of India's most well-known student of psychoanalysis: Sudhir Kakar. Among other things, his work deals with the erotic and sexual lives of Indian women. Arguing that in the context of the extended Hindu family, eroticism is called into the service of preserving the lineage, he notes that women's sexuality rarely finds expression with this context. Hedged in by familial norms and demands, the woman's erotic charge rarely finds a site for play, until the birth of a male child. Then follows an intense phase in her life, when she looms as the most significant figure in the infant's life, exuding energy and power which appears potent and suffocating at the same time. This early bonding with an all-consuming mother, observes Kakar, is retained as an ambivalent memory in the adult male, who now comes to view all women as devouring and dangerous.

The arguments of Dinnerstein—and to an extent, Kakar—have the same demerits as Freud. They are profoundly ahistorical, and besides, make women almost entirely culpable for their own subordination. There is also no explanation as to how little boys who feel helpless before and resentful of their mothers go on to construct complex social systems which subordinate women. What are the economic structures and social customs which make this possible?

Additionally, Kakar's ideal family is clearly a specific social type, more prevalent in parts of northern India than elsewhere. In Bengal, for instance, the same all-consuming mother becomes an object of desire, with men confessing that they wished to be like them, in fact would avidly desire to turn female. Thus wrote Girindrasekhar Bose, founder of the Indian Psychoanalytic Association to Freud. Bose said that in India the Oedipus Complex did not seem to exist in quite the same way as it did in the societies that Freud analysed. This was because unlike in

Europe, femininity was not fundamentally rejected. The plethora of goddesses worshipped in Bengal, noted Bose, testified to a cultural veneration of the female principle. That is, men did not grow up with the complex ambivalence towards women that Freud discovered in his patients, rather they desired the mother, but were not afflicted either by jealousy or disgust. Instead they actively sought her powers out and desired to be imbued with her energies.

SEXUALITY AND SUBORDINATION

Public debates around sexuality and power in modern India emerged in the wake of an articulate women's movement. Prior to that, Gandhi spoke and wrote incessantly about the perils of uncontrolled lust. His writings on this subject may be read as incipient theories of masculine sexuality, but they are far too embedded within his ethical universe to amount to anything more than appendices to his highly suggestive ideas on power and renunciation. The women's movement's engagement with sexuality happened in the 1980s with the infamous rape of a 14-year-old tribal girl by two police constables. The incident acquired a certain notoriety after the trial court acquitted the policemen, on the argument that the girl was used to sex and there was nothing to prove that the constables were indeed to be blamed. This verdict which was upheld by a higher court served as a catalyst to bring into existence a dormant feminist sensibility on the subject of sexual violence.

The terms of discourse, as they were outlined by various women's groups, identified sexual violence as an expression of power. They also pointed out that in a context of power, neither a woman's prior sexual history nor the question of her consent to the vile act are relevant. Sexual violence, it was argued, could not be explained in terms of male lust or desire, either. It was the ultimate act of male terror, meant to intimidate and silence the victim.

Discussions of sexual violence enabled women to name the routine hurt and abuse they suffered within the family. Women could now discuss the emotional and sexual traumas they experienced within marriage and in the extended family without fear of being stigmatized for daring to discuss their personal experiences. Flavia Agnes' poignant account of domestic violence and how she freed herself from an unhappy marriage captures the bitterness and anguish of women who now possessed the discursive means and political support to voice their hurt.

Two major responses to the debates on sexual violence appeared in the mid-1980s: the one, articulated by women's groups that were self-consciously feminist and committed to a politics of resisting male sexual authority and violence, sought to counter these latter through feminist counselling. Support centres for victims of sexual and other forms of violence emerged in major cities. Feminists viewed counselling as both therapeutic and political. They sought to instil self-confidence and self-respect in women, who felt humiliated and guilty for having been assaulted. But feminists also felt that their work possessed other dimensions. They were calling social attention to abusive acts which encapsulated the worst forms of patriarchal power.

The other response emerged in the context of debates about sexual violence in a feudal-caste-religious context, where men held their honour and their community honour dear and inscribed these on the bodies of their women. Thus, protecting a woman's chastity or sexually assaulting a woman were seen as tantamount to preserving and desecrating male honour and caste or religious identity respectively. Caste and religious riots happened at regular intervals throughout the late 1980s and after, and women were often the locus of events—as victims, as points of reference in violent assertions of caste identity or religious fervour. Feminists working with the rural poor or with dalits or adivasis, or with victims of riots, saw in sexual violence a specific and gendered expression of authority that was committed to preserving a hierarchical and unjust social order. They pointed out that the bodies of women constituted the sites on which patriarchal quarrels about identity and power, oppression and resistance were fought out.

Two important essays are relevant in this context. Gail Omvedt's monograph on violence and Vasanth and Kalpana Kannabiran's essay on gender, sexuality and caste violence. In different ways, these writers examine the forms and modalities of sexual assault in a society deeply fissured by caste and class—in terms of how these differences shape masculine and feminine self-perceptions, how and where caste identity intersects and informs a person's sense of being male and female.

These debates about sexuality posed the following question: Is sexual violence separable from the uneven economic, social and familial structures from which it emerges, in other words, does it possess its own intrinsic logic? This was the question that Catharine MacKinnon and others articulated, though to different ends and purposes. In the Indian context, this question was addressed primarily to parties that called themselves communist and which were watchful and sceptical of these developments in the Indian women's movements. Lively and acrimonious debates followed, with the left parties unwilling to concede that the question of women's sexual subordination need not be discussed solely in the terms of the class struggle.

Around the same time, that is, during the late 1980s and after, female sexuality became a subject of debate in two interlinked contexts: on reproductive technology and female health. Feminists questioned sharply the government's health policies that reduced female health to reproductive health. They spoke of the need for women to know and heal their bodies themselves. On one hand, women's groups outlined an uncompromising critique of contraceptive technology that was clearly unfriendly to women and destructive of their health. On the other hand, several alternative health strategies were outlined, workshops on natural healing traditions were organized. These discussions enabled exchanges on a range of female bodily concerns, besides medical and therapeutic issues: from sexual need and pleasure to the experience of motherhood.

These various debates on sexuality tacitly raised questions about the making of gender identities and the institution of gender norms: firstly, they outlined the various social, cultural and economic structures which determine and influence the constitution of male and female subjects. Secondly, they called into question traditional notions of femininity, both through criticisms of existing practices and an emerging feminist politics. These observations and criticisms looked to resolutions within the framework of law and governance. That is, they did not lead to more sustained theory-making on issues of sexuality and power, or on the nature of sexuality, the existence of sexual preferences.

There was, however, a marked shift in the mid-1990s, when sexuality as an integral area of experience became the focus of discussion. Rather than contextualize sexual concerns within the terms of larger social structures, some feminist thinkers and activists attempted to read social and economic life in and through experiences and narratives of sexuality. This development coincided with and was anticipated by the emergence of articulate gay and lesbian groups which brought a different theoretical emphasis to discussions on sexuality: questions of sexual choice, the personal and social implications of these choices. These debates re-focused feminist attention on modes of growing up, socialization and the pressures exerted by gender norms.

SUMMING UP

In the first three chapters we looked critically at ideas about gender. Whether it is a religious idea, a belief in the notion that men and women possess innate qualities or the everyday acceptance of social roles, we saw that human beings subscribed to these ideas because the cost of not subscribing, of nonconformity was and is very high. But we also saw, in Chapter 4, how these ideas are not unchanging ones. They do change and are transformed by inventive and ingenious human beings who engage with ideas in an active, dynamic sense. Ideas about gender, we found out, are formed through interpretation and contestation, that is, neither men nor women surrender away their distinctive notions of what they think of masculine and feminine virtues. They battle it out, as Proudhon and Deroin did; often men emerged the victors, not because they knew better but as we learnt in this chapter, they possessed greater power, better access to education and ideas.

In this chapter, we saw how the making of masculinity and femininity came about, how and why women came to be more or less exclusively identified with motherhood and child-care, and men with work, intelligence and power. We know that a sexual division of labour came to exist in society, determining male and female identities, spaces, work and destinies. Historians and theorists do not agree on why such a division came to be.

For Engels, the sexual division of labour seemed an outgrowth of a natural division of labour which gradually came to be used against women. For feminist theorists, who wrote after him, nature played a role in dividing tasks, only with respect to the specific act of childbearing. They argued there was nothing natural about women being confined to the household. This happened because they became objects of exchange and because of abduction and rape. For Freud and Freudians, girls take to mothering and child-care because their psychic development pushes them towards these tasks, likewise, boys are pushed to assume public roles and responsibilities. Feminist historians claim that the sexual division of labour took place because men managed to gain control over women's reproductive powers, rendering women powerless and dependent on their sexual ties with men for any sort of achievement or growth. American feminists of the 1970s argued that it was the nature of the sexual relationship between men and women, its very dynamics, that was responsible for women being so crushed by patriarchy.

All historical explanations of gender are agreed on one fact; masculinity and femininity are not eternal, given norms. They were elaborated, institutionalized and made to seem eternal, to justify the power and authority which men enjoyed at the expense of women. This power and authority exists at several levels: the economic, the sexual, the social and the psychic.

Now we have before us both descriptions—and criticisms–of commonplace assumptions about masculinity and femininity, as well as historical accounts of the making of masculine and feminine identities. The question before us is how to use gender as a tool of analysis, in a way that helps us understand the world around us, enables us make sense of our own lives.

Postscript: The Uses of History

Using historical accounts of gender to grasp the world around us is a complex task. Firstly, the theories we discussed, sketch in broad bold strokes the key elements of the reality they examine. They give us the conceptual tools to identify and trace out the skeletal structure of the worlds we inhabit. But they do not tell us, in so many words, how and through what particular means are women, for instance, persuaded that beauty and sexual appeal are their most valuable assets. Secondly, they do not explain at length how entire systems of law, custom and ideas evolved to define and justify masculine and feminine norms. Yet theories of the history of gender are what we begin with. They contain the thread which we unwind, as we explore the labyrinthine nature of the societies we live in, where every path we trace out diverges into myriad others, to either intersect with or run parallel to other paths we are yet to explore.

An exploration of teenage sexuality, for instance, based on the Freudian notions of psychic development may initially take us through the path of family relationships, which, then diverges into other domains: the sexual, the emotional, the communicative, the fantastic, on the one hand. On the other, it takes us through school rooms, playgrounds, peer groups, and so on. As we try and understand sexuality in and through all these contexts, we are bound to identify both common assumptions as well as the contradictory messages the teenager receives, understand that family and school may reinforce certain notions, while the world outside contradicts these, say, through media images. As we assemble our evidence and arguments, we will come up against the fact that theories work only to the extent they explain the reality they set out to examine. If this reality is not graspable within the context of the theory, then it is clear the theory itself needs to be interrogated, some of its premises re-examined and altered, if necessary.

The point is, no theory in itself is exhaustive or entirely adequate to the tasks we set it. A theory assumes its characteristic form and meaning through the specific uses we find for it. For example, if we wish to apply the Marxist theory of the sexual division of labour in the Indian context, we need to look at the sexual division of labour in relation to caste, on the one hand, and forms of the Indian family, on the other. Thus we need to find out how the caste system affects and shapes the sexual division of labour. Are women consigned to domestic work in all the castes? Is their identity shaped by the general caste labour they perform, or by their sexual identities? Do the structure and emotional content of Indian family life feed into or subvert the sexual division of labour? Is parenting an exclusively female activity in India? Are young men everywhere encouraged to pay more attention to production, or the sphere of public work rather than the family? Does the sexual division of labour work against all women in the same family? What role does age have to play in the assignment of work to women?

Are historical accounts of gender useful in comprehending only obviously gendered realities, such as sexuality and childhood, or can they prove illuminating with respect to realities which are clearly not marked by gender, such as poverty, for instance? How does one use gender as a category of analysis in this context?

At one level, poverty appears a great equalizer—both men and women are poor. But if we look at what poverty actually entails for women, we get a different picture. For example, if a limited amount of food is available, the woman of the family eats last. If a poor family has to exercise a choice about sending a boy or a girl child to school, they usually settle the matter in favour of the boy.

Let us take another situation: caste and social justice. Here again it may seem that general educational deprivation and social injustice are common to both men and women amongst the lower and deprived castes. While this is generally true, it is also equally true that when these castes are provided with affirmative laws to better their prospects, men, rather than women, are likely to take advantage of things like reservation in educational institutions and government posts for backward classes (as backward but not dalit castes are called). During the entire debate about reservations for the backward classes during the 1980s in India, not many asked if women from these castes would benefit equally from the proposed measure. It was assumed that social justice was a gender-neutral idea. In other words, the typical backward class person was imaged as male, in spite of the fact that one of the criteria for determining backwardness is the educational status of women in a particular caste or backward class group. Thus no one insisted that a crucial component of affirmative action should be gender justice, so that as many women as men would benefit.

Finally, to be able to use gender effectively as a tool of analysis, a category that illuminates the reality we wish to study, we need to understand that reality as dynamic. When we identify and isolate elements of a reality, for instance, sexuality or socialization, we must keep in mind that in these spheres of human activity, as in any other, human beings act within specific social and economic structures and contexts—the nuclear family, a market economy, a culture marked by sexual reticence that is expressed through customs and practices, and so on. The norms which direct and influence human behaviour are directly or indirectly related to these structures, sometimes they appear as directives, other times as tacit rules which everybody agrees to abide by. Actual human behaviour attempts to negotiate between structure, norm and individual desire, sometimes leaning more heavily on one, sometimes on the other. That is to say, in any given society, structures, norms and action based on those norms exist in a tense, uneven and even contradictory relationship. In every instance, we need to establish the coordinates to this relationship, and find out what prevails in the final instance and why, how particular or general is the phenomena we have observed, what accounts for the difference, if any.

By thus historicizing and contextualizing a theory, we breathe life into it, render it dynamic. Theory ceases to be abstract and becomes flexible, it takes on the grit of the every day, the rich texture of individual lives. Theories of gender have necessarily to wind their way through complex and often unpredictable realities, and often the observations and the links we make as we study and criticize render the theory supple.

6

Gender Practices

In the previous chapters, we looked at masculinity and femininity in the context of specific ideas on the one hand, and as a feature of historical development on the other. Ideas, we realized, are real, possess real effects. Yet they do not exist by themselves, specific social and economic structures which had evolved over a period of time have given birth to and structured these ideas. Now it remains to be seen how ideas are actualized in practice, what makes a certain norm work in a specific circumstance and why. In this section, we will look at some commonplace injunctions about masculinity and femininity and trace out the dense network of people and systems through which ideas are experienced, accepted or rejected.

Before we set out exploring these injunctions that we receive, interpret and live out, as men and women, we need to be clear about two things. Firstly, though gender differences reflect and express complex economic and social relationships of power, they are also lived differences, that is, norms of masculinity and femininity are real and experienced as real by most of us. We do not see in them a configuration of power and authority. Secondly, gender differences are crucial to human relationships, in fact, gender, as such, supposes and implies a relationship. When we refer to masculinity and femininity, we refer not to two unrelated categories but to two inextricably and intimately linked ones. Men and women accept or subvert norms in the immediate context of their relationship to each other.

Gender relationships involve intimacies and enmities; love and hatred, affection and violence, power and abjection, hurt and surrender. Human beings play out their destinies in and through a combination of these emotions and the acts which are inspired by them. They also come to and acquire a sense of themselves, their needs and desires in the course of living these relationships. To understand those affective and experiential elements which are central to human self-perceptions—as men or women—we need to identify those qualities and acts which mark men and women as different and yet complementary. Most of these qualities and acts are aspects of our physical existence; that is, we feel, are and live as men and women, or as neither, in and through our bodies. In this sense, the human body is not only corporeal, it also becomes the locus of sexual identity, of familial and social roles, as well as sexual self-awareness and expectations. We may thus profitably examine expressions of gender which revolve around the human body to understand how and why it is so difficult—and yet necessary—to challenge given notions of masculinity and femininity.

Common and even routine expressions of gender are centred on what we shall refer to as practices of the body: whether this has to do with how we look, that is, the means through which we seek to express our femaleness or maleness; or with experiences of the body, such as sexual love, sport, religion; or with injunctions to the body, notions of discipline, restraint, control.

The human body is schooled into looking, acting, desiring, expressing and controlling its movements in a certain way through a range of institutions and agents (people who actually direct and lead others or seek to influence them) as well as ideas and beliefs. The family, school, media, religious and cultural organizations, and within these, individuals, such as parents, teachers, peers, religious leaders, cultural icons, like film or rock stars, provide norms, role models as well as exercise power and influence over us. We also respond to ideas implicit in and expressed as custom, myth, ritual, in art, literature and music.

For our purposes, I propose to look at the schooling of the body in terms of appearance, experience and discipline. In the context of gender, these would translate into Norms of Male and Female Beauty; Norms of Sexuality and Motherhood and Norms of Control. I propose to demonstrate how these norms are actualized, and identify crucial and important institutions and ideas which enable this actualization.

APPEARANCE

Very few people seriously dispute a widely accepted notion: that beauty becomes a woman, whereas virility becomes a man. Widely different cultures subscribe to this maxim. The idea may be found, in one form or another, at several periods in human history. Why was it—and is—deemed important for women to look beautiful and men to be virile? At its simplest, beauty as a physical marker distinguishes women from men—women are those who take great care over their appearance, whereas men care chiefly about their prowess, the energy and ability that allows them to do and act as they wish. But beauty and virility possess other meanings as well.

The Body Beautiful

Notions of beauty are normative, that is, they exist as rules, even imperatives to which the woman's body must adhere. These rules change from time to time and are varied. In all circumstances, and in all historical epochs, they are directed at women from the outside. Yet women accept, respond enthusiastically to, and actualize these rules—sometimes even creating the conditions in which a particular set of rules may be re-made.

Who makes these beauty rules? Often beauty rules do

not exist in themselves. They are expressed as aspects of a feminine ideal that all women ought necessarily to want to emulate. This ideal, in turn, is defined, framed and expressed in the art, literature, law and culture of a particular historical epoch. Paintings, drawings, sculpture and literary representations of women comprise the most obvious expressions of this idea. If we are to review critically the literature or art of a period for the feminine ideal it upheld, we would find that in almost all instances this ideal had been articulated by men. Let us take European pictorial art as an example. Whether the feminine ideal was defined throughout the image of Mary, mother of God, or through various queens and aristocratic women, it was men—artists and sculptors—who fashioned the ideal. And it was these men, and the patrons who supported their work, who set standards and measures of female beauty.

What were these standards based on? In some instances, on contemporary notions of perfection, which often had to do with symmetry of form, colour, and so on. In some cases, standards of beauty derived from character: Mary, mother of God, was both good and beautiful. Or, conversely, real beauty was believed to express itself through goodness. Others held that beauty can only be measured through the purpose it served. If beauty induced lust or encouraged lasciviousness, then it was not considered true beauty. If, on the other hand, beauty called attention to a woman's modesty, chastity and goodness of temper, it was to be honoured. Sometimes, beauty was also defined in a differentiated sort of way, that is, several measures were employed even within the same historical period. Thus there was the shy beauty of the bride, the brazen beauty of the seductress, the regal air which marked queenly good looks.

Fundamentally, though, beauty was a product of ideas and opinions, entertained and expressed by men about women. Measures of beauty were outlined and framed by their brushes, chisels and pens. In this sense, we may say that the ideal of female beauty expressed in European pictorial art, though diverse, was framed by the 'male gaze'. The male gaze treated women as objects. Women's beauty was an object for male creativity and imagination to shape, manipulate and transform. Men were driven thus to objectify women by felt notions of pleasure, gratification and desire.

What granted men the power and, more important, the authority to thus view women as objects? The power they wielded in real life—as fathers, husbands, noblemen, kings—and the access they enjoyed to education and the learning of the creative arts. In this sense, the male gaze may be said to represent the visceral, emotional and psychological expression of male authority, the crucial node in the complex network of relationships which characterize patriarchal society.

Women, socially powerless, and lacking the means to express themselves, consented to be these objects, thus submitting themselves to beauty rules in whose making they had played almost no role. Fixed in a range of roles and ideals which served as veritable mirrors in which they were asked to view themselves, women learnt to recognize and accept these various beauty norms as their own. That is, they imagined them to be given, possessing universal value. The male gaze triumphed precisely on this account: by establishing itself as a way of seeing and framing that is natural to the human eye. The male gaze is not peculiar to Europe. It may be found in all cultures. This is not surprising, since in almost all cultures, men, rather than women, had access to learning and the arts.

In our own time, both in India and elsewhere, the fashion industry, media personalities and media representations embody and express the power of the male gaze. They create role models, urge women to look this way and that, promote products which, they claim, will enhance or even enable one to be beautiful. The norms set by those in the beauty business serve to define not only the most beautiful woman in the world, but also offer a particular definition of femininity. In this instance, the ideal feminine type is thin, elegant, works hard to be beautiful, diets, exercises, is not averse to intelligent conversation, but is not on that account an intellectual woman, loves to do charity, and ultimately longs to settle into a marriage of love. This ideal is both contemporary and historical. It is powerful and appealing, because it aligns traditional feminine attributes to a modern purpose, while emphasizing that though women today are prone to show off their bodies, they are, nonetheless what women have always been: home-makers.

The creation of such ideals and norms is seldom a one-way process. As we have just noted, women consent to be objects, in fact, seek out this object status. For example, the 'Miss Universe' body ideal that was so assiduously cultivated by the media in urban India during the mid-1990s was eagerly and avidly consumed by tens of thousands of young middle class and lower middle class urbanites and suburbanites growing up in the shadow of the American fashion and entertainment industry. These young women had come of age at a time when India was busy integrating its economy into the global market. Western cosmetics were now widely and easily available, so was Western television. The thin emaciated look favoured by international fashion designers—one of whom claimed that a body was merely a hanger for her garment creations to be displayed to advantage—soon became popular among a class of teenagers here. The fashion and media interests encouraged and applauded this popular interest in an ideal that had originally been fashioned in North America. They organized and supported contests and events around this new beauty norm.

The point is, women and girls, by actively desiring a certain sort of body or particular image, participate in the making of beauty norms. Ultimately, of course, the fashion and media industry gain a great deal out of the beauty business. Yet we cannot discount the role of individual women and girls who endorse and buy into these beauty norms and thereby actualize and perpetrate them. This has remained a vexed question with feminists: Are women victims of the beauty business or collaborators? Historically, notions of female beauty have served to render women as objects—of male desire, consumption and use. Yet given their general state of powerlessness, women have used their status as objects to gain favour with men and acquire a measure of power and authority for themselves.

Feminists argue that the ideal of beauty has to be viewed as a construction, a myth imposed on women. They claim that this myth serves a particular purpose in patriarchal society. For one, it divides women into the pleasing and the plain. In a context where so-called plain looks are considered valueless and, worse, a disadvantage for women, all women aspire to re-make themselves. Those who cannot live up to the norm are afflicted with a sense of inadequacy, guilt and jealousy, and most of all a corrosive anxiety that they would meet with male disapproval and indifference.

This is something quite commonplace: one has only to examine critically advertisements for cosmetics to realize how both copy and image respond with fine precision to these fears and anxieties. Though the product advertised may be anything—soap, perfume, deodorant—the message often has less to do with a particular product's worth, than with how it enables one to appear confident and poised about one's appearance. Copy and image also imply that if one did not use such and such product, one will have to live with fear, of being left out of the beauty race, ignored and teased. A mesh of emotions, ideas and institutions thus help to cajole subtly, threaten and convince women that a certain sort of beauty ideal is essential to and even fundamental to their sense of themselves as worthy persons.

The beauty ideal impinges on female identity in another fundamental way. It enables women to delight intensely in their becoming objects of the male gaze. That is, women assume their object status with pleasure, as if it became them. The question of their desire, their subjectivity, is thus resolved within the terms of pleasure and power contained in the male gaze. Thus, in some instances, women even claim that they can best realize themselves through an active and defiant cultivation of their bodily good looks. Others, especially beauty queens and fashion models, have gone a step further: they maintain that they experience a measure of individual freedom in thus expressing themselves.

These experiences of power and freedom are by no means false as the adherence to the beauty norm does confer power and privilege to those who practise it. Moreover, as just noted, women have historically utilized their beauty to attain positions of authority and power. Yet both the freedom and power thus cultivated by women are severely circumscribed, for they are to be enjoyed only for a very short time. For beauty is feted, praised and adored as long as the flush of youth remains. As a woman ages, she is not considered fit enough to represent the beauty whims of the season. Besides, the experience of freedom and power, even during the short enchanted moment that it lasts, comes with a price. The body has to be tutored, disciplined, and manipulated in accordance with norms that may or may not afford oneself health or comfort. Finally, a woman feels empowered and free by transforming herself into an object. In the process, she fails to see that she is really not making a choice, but merely working a pre-given and limited role to advantage.

Of course, not all social institutions and individuals are equally convinced of or impressed by ideals of beauty as they obtain in a particular moment in history. Thus, at any given time, there may exist competing definitions of beauty. For instance, certain sections of the media, such as those which cater to family interests and audiences, may re-define the beauty norm. Rather than grant total and unqualified support to the body beautiful, they may insist on judging a girl and woman through other measures. Housekeeping skills, modesty, patience may all be called into the service of re-defining the beauty ideal. Likewise, religious institutions may declare an obsession with the body as sinful, an example of selfish absorption in oneself. Rather—and they would argue thus—beauty consists in being simple and selfless, in ideals of quiet charity.

Yet even those who reject the beauty ideal and seek to define femaleness in terms of character and inner worth seldom dispute the idea that beauty is central to experiences and expressions of womanhood. They may speak instead of inner beauty, the beauty that lies at the heart of goodness, in the clarity of the mind or in the piety of the soul. Nor do these dissenting ideals of beauty question the manner in which a woman's sense of herself is almost always linked to her ability to make herself into an object, for approval by and for the enjoyment and pleasure of men.

On the other hand, feminism has created a discursive and political space for the active critique of beauty, whether as myth, big business or an object of the male gaze. Likewise, a radical culture of homosexuality, with its emphasis on same-sex love and comradeship, has deconstructed the very notion of the male gaze, though in some instances, homosexual couples, like men and women, construct themselves as active and passive partners. Yet expressions of homosexual love do attempt to transcend that objectification of the (female) body which is central to everyday romance. They do this through a range of strategies: individualistic celebrations of the body; a non-monogamous sexual philosophy and chiefly through expressions of non-genital sexuality. Male and female bodies thus enter into relationships without their genital identities being central to their coming together.

Mark of a Man

Male virility possesses a different social and individual response. If beauty is a norm constructed by the male gaze, virility is an ideal, a norm that emerges from within the masculine body. It is as if virility is a condition of maleness, in an obvious organic sort of way. Thus virility is an ideal that encourages, enables an expression outwards. It calls for the male body to forge ahead, pursue adventure and heroic action, seek sexual pleasure and satisfaction, conquest and power. Unlike the beauty ideal which demands that women transform themselves into objects, and which coaxes women to measure themselves against an external norm, virility persuades men to be subjects of their destiny, urges them towards active secular and social self-expression.

Once again the example of European art is instructive. Male figures, whether in painting or sculpture, are seldom passive. They are almost always dynamic: doing, performing, suffering, in short, acting out their desires and will. Female figures, to reiterate a point made earlier, are passive objects meant to kindle a range of emotions in the predominantly male viewer: from the maternal to the carnal.

It is not accidental that non-virile men are viewed as suffering from an inner lack. They are usually considered maimed, disabled and feminine. Women who are not and who do not aspire to be beautiful are not seen as internally lacking; they are unpleasant to the viewing male eye, objects of fun and satire, creatures who embody wickedness and evil. That is, ugly women are seen both as subversive of the male gaze—hence they have to be mocked—and threatening, hence the insinuation of evil.

In our contemporary world, the male body too has been consigned to object status. Men appear in advertisements, revealing their bodies, showing off a fine back or a pair of strong legs. Yet, male identity is not exclusively dependent on their looks, it continues to be an adjunct of the power they enjoy and experience. So-called ugly men can still find themselves beautiful wives, for the measure of their success or importance is not their looks. Rather it is their wealth and power. This brings us to a rather important social truth: male virility is a measure of the actual authority men enjoy, enforce and sustain. Men are expected to express themselves through physical—and other—acts of heroism and adventure, through their forays into the outer world, because they are seen as natural heirs to authority, just as women are viewed as naturally passive and susceptible to being objects. Clearly, beauty and virility are not mere attributes through which we recognize the quintessential feminine and masculine. Rather, they are the means through which women and men express and experience themselves. Besides, they underlie male-female interactions and affect their most intimate encounters with each other.

How do women and men experience this identity, both in relationship to themselves and to each other? Before we go on to consider this question, we need to understand that masculinity is neither cohesive nor consistent. It is always constructed, made to seem powerful and the norm. This of course implies that such a norm does not exist naturally and has to be articulated forcibly. This is because, as we saw, many men simply cannot afford to be masculine in the way we have described it. This is because they are not powerful, being lower class, lower caste and poor. Or it could be because they are not considered or do not consider themselves to be typically masculine: gay men, for instance, or men who are shy, gentle, retiring; or because they are the wrong colour; as blacks, or browns or other non-white colours, they are more or less masculine, but never the norm.

EXPERIENCE

Beauty and virility and a range of other emotions and attributes associated with them are central to the way we experience ourselves. They construct us as human beings who possess certain kinds of bodies, destined to play out certain sorts of roles. They grant meaning to our sense of our own bodies, shape and influence our sexual lives.

The Experiences of Femininity

The male gaze images women as objects of both pleasure and use. Women's bodies are to yield to men's needs. However, these needs are complex. Men desire women as lovers, wives, mothers of their children, whores, aesthetic objects, ideals. These desires elicit and demand different sorts of female bodies (and beauties). Generally, though, in most cultures, the beauty ideal translates itself into two distinctive yet paired types: the wife and the concubine, the lover and the vamp, the good woman and the bad woman. That is, female beauty is granted two markets; the licit and the illicit. Licit beauty is tame, regular, passive; illicit beauty, wild, sensuous, seductive and aggressive. The one is meant for domestic conjugal use, pleasure and significance, linked to marriage and motherhood. The other is in fact a public beauty—indicating sexual availability, a dangerous female power and bearing the marks of the forbidden.

The male gaze has so imprinted itself on all our major social, cultural and religious institutions that the norms of femininity are defined, interpreted and expressed chiefly through this paired idea, though in real life, women's roles and functions are diverse and answer a variety of male and female needs. But whether it is folklore, literature, religious tales, art, sculpture, the plots of theatre and cinema: the paired ideal, of the good wife and the seductive mistress, may be found in all of them. In some representations, the non-domestic female body may be accorded a tender and sympathetic treatment, in others, it may be castigated as evil and sinful. In some, the good, dutiful body of the wife may be made to undergo terrible privations, while the bad, beautiful body of the witch or the dancer may revel in its own sensuousness. All sorts of combinations exist, some more nuanced, some less so. In some, the line dividing the paired ideal is rather thin, a phenomenon that we observe in the American star Madonna; or in our own context, in the film heroines of the 1990s in Hindi and Tamil cinema and theatre.

The paired ideal is significant in another respect: it suggests a norm and a deviation from the norm. In fact, the norm and its deviation, the wife and the mistress, or the lover and the vamp, are defined in mutual terms. The licit/illicit basis to this pairing is central to the way several societies order their conjugal and familial lives. In several parts of India, for instance, a good family is defined as one where the women of the family are honourable, that is, where they guard their chastity with their very lives. The chaste wife is so essential to her family's stability, that she is often enjoined to remain indulgent towards her husband, even if he were wayward and promiscuous, because if she were to nag, complain or leave him, the family would be plunged into disrepute. Conversely, she is raised on stories of sexually violated women killing themselves out of shame, suffering enormous guilt and going mad. She is told of what happens to women who desire too much, whether food, clothing or sex. That is, she is schooled not only to be a good and loyal wife, but also not to be a woman who is the very obverse of the good woman. All this affects her sense of self profoundly, as we shall soon see.

Since the beginning of the modern world, from at least the time of the French Revolution of 1789 and the coming of the industrial revolution, the roles and functions available to women changed dramatically. This happened in different ways and at different paces throughout the world. In all those contexts where the effects of the French and industrial revolutions were felt, new ideas of democracy, female equality and female economic independence combined to produce new role models for women. Women could now actually find work in distant towns and factories, where they were paid a wage that reduced their dependence on men's income. The new culture of democracy enabled them to think through the question of their rights. Women workers, intellectuals, artists, women who started cooperatives, trade unions, through their lives, work and struggles embodied a new female ideal, animated by female self-worth, independence, sexual daring and a desire to change the world, to make it more egalitarian, for both men and women. More important, they could stand the beauty ideal on its head, challenge and mock at a male gaze which was content to image women as passive and malleable.

The new ideal though required courage and energy. Some women found both, inspired by new found solidarities that were forged between women in trade unions, reading clubs, friendships, through letters, shared ideas and interests. Others found themselves in radical political circles which accepted them, though at times radical men too were bewildered and even annoyed by the self-assurance and earnest desire to know and act which these women exhibited. But for many others, this ideal appeared threatening. It simply demanded too much from them. For as the historian Gerda Lerner has pointed out, intelligent and self-confident women stood to lose the love of the men in their lives. Though there were supportive fathers and husbands, they remained exceptions. Several women who staked claims to equality and independence, who announced themselves to be feminists had to struggle with men—fathers, brothers, lovers, husbands. Then, there was also the problem of economic independence. To live by a profession, a skill demanded a high degree of confidence and for many women, used to finding economic security within marriage, this option did not appear attractive. Even working class women, at times, wished to exchange their everyday labour and drudgery for the security and comforts of conjugal and familial existence.

Thus, even today, nearly two centuries and more after the modern world emerged, the new feminine-feminist ideal has not won for itself a great many converts. Women's sense of self continues to be influenced, even determined by the old, paired ideal. As we have noted earlier, women are fundamentally anxious, tentative about themselves. Would their looks please or escape notice? If they do not fall in love and cannot marry, what is to become of them? What awaits a woman if she cannot attain wifehood and motherhood?

The anxieties of women are compounded by the fact that they cannot view themselves, experience themselves, without being reminded of the ultimate destinies which await their bodies. Besides, as we have said earlier, they are haunted, troubled, and compelled to adhere to those functions and destinies allocated to them by the threat of dishonour. They dare not think intimate, significant thoughts about their needs and desires, for fear of becoming those 'other' women, who are always what they are not. Thus, the desire to please and be pleasing, and the anxieties which accompany this desire persuade women, in fact, enable them actively to seek out romance, marriage and childbearing as much desired vocations.

The question arises: are these anxieties and this desire to please and answer to the needs of the male gaze common to all women? What about poor, lower caste and working class women? The lives of poor, labouring women revolve around work and survival. For many of them, their bodies are instruments of work. It is not that working class, lower caste women do not delight in colour, texture, in the aesthetic. But looking beautiful is always an indulgence, an act of luxury they reserve for themselves when they have extra time and money. Though they do make themselves up into figures that seek to elicit approval from men, there is also a certain self-delighting quality to their desire to look pretty. More fundamentally, though, their bodies are as bound to defined roles and functions. They are expected to love, marry and bear children and suffer great sorrow if this destiny veers away from them. The conditions of their existence, one of survival and labour, however, mediate their experience of love, sexuality and work.

Work is central to their lives, inextricably linked to being alive, being able to feed their children. Work allows even the most wretched of working women to experience a sense of her skill, her self-sufficiency, feelings that are alien and threatening to middle class women. This necessarily influences working women's attitudes towards love and sexual desire. They are less troubled by notions of womanly and familial honour. This does not mean that they are habitually sexually free or daring. Their status as workers, visible in the public world, renders them sexually vulnerable. This vulnerability becomes part of the conditions under which they labour, hence they set no special premium on their sexuality. They know that it can be abused. As dalit women say ironically and sadly, their bodies are seldom untouchable to landlords and contractors who employ them, though these men otherwise practise untouchability.

On the other hand, working class, lower caste women do feel empowered to walk out of unhappy marriages in the confidence that they can support themselves. They may feel as committed to marriage and motherhood, but when they think they have a choice, they walk away more easily and with less guilt from a situation of violence and indifference. A common faith and commitment to motherhood, however, may be seen to inspire women across classes and communities. We shall shortly consider why this should be so.

ROMANCE MARRIAGE AND MOTHERHOOD

Let us examine a little closely women's sense of romance, marriage and motherhood. In the Indian context, romantic fantasies are fulsomely and unashamedly expressed in and through the medium of cinema. It is film that has granted voice, style, gesture and content to modern Indian notions of romance. Likewise, it is film that provides enabling wifely and maternal role models. This does not mean that real life imitates cinema or that cinema accurately reflects existing gender sensibilities. Films constitute an important expression of social consciousness, resonate in complex ways to feel social needs and aspirations. In this qualified sense, films grant us clues about how a society publicly thinks out its positions on gender.

Romance in Indian cinema centres around that peculiar thing, 'body chemistry'. The camera attempts to capture the play of this chemistry in any number of inventive ways. In the early and middle decades of Indian cinema as well as in the late twentieth century, the camera performed to a certain grammar. For the young woman, romance was and still is possible and exciting only under conditions of subterfuge and dissimulation. The audience willingly suspends disbelief, accepting and enjoying what, in real life, they would baulk at—in the secure knowledge that the surreptitious coming together of lovers augurs a happy and legitimate marriage and the restoration of order, at the end of the film. However, this aura of subterfuge communicates to the young female viewer a model of female desire that is furtive, afraid, and yet secretly—or brazenly—lustful. Tainted with the whiff of the forbidden, the woman—both the character in the film and the viewer—anticipates with excitement and delight the mysteries of conjugal love. The film takes the viewer and the character through a tortuous plot that ends on an amicable note. Meanwhile, the female viewer is left with the sense that her own being has to be carefully preserved through romance and lust for the chaste marriage bed.

The point is that romance in the Indian context is necessarily shrouded in secrecy and guilt. It induces desire, lust and longing, but ultimately refuses to grant these emotions any validity, unless they are expressed in the context of future conjugality. Thus the experience of marriage becomes central to female sexual discovery, and often this proves to be traumatic. This is not only because many young brides are uninformed about sexual love, but because it binds them to a relationship they cannot easily refute. For, intimacies, especially sexual and erotic ones, can be imagined, experienced and rendered legitimate only within marriage. This, in turn, means that no bride can afford to desert her marriage, even if it proves to be abusive, because in her sense of it such a desertion connotes a betrayal of her own body, its sexual trust and intimacy.

Such a knowledge of her sexuality allows the young bride very few options; she dare not desire in ways that may subvert the sanctity of her marriage bed. Further, she cannot, must not, voice out her displeasure or hurt over her husband's sexual behaviour. Above all, she has to live with the burden of a bound sexuality. This knowledge of herself and the multiple material burdens that wifedom thrusts on her together make the young bride's life harsh, painful and sad. Of course, no woman accepts her position as such—there are bound to be negotiations, subtle threats, refusals on her part as well. But the point is the logic of the male gaze works such that destined to marry, she cannot escape her sexual fate.

Once again, we may look to film for productive instances of how women are enabled and enable themselves to lead the lives they do. Recently, the notion of romance has undergone several changes in Indian cinema, but marriage continues to be viewed in the ideal light that had been reserved for it, from very early on. This is more so for women than men. Even in movies that push romance to the edge, portraying sexually defiant heroines and pathological and obsessive heroes, the romantic heroine is ultimately re-figured as the dutiful, loving, self-abnegating wife. At a more inchoate level of consciousness, women experience their status as wives as precious and mysterious, since it is their only access to sexual love and the intimacies it fosters. Whatever be their actual experiences of this love, they surround it with a certain aura that renders the married state extremely desirable.

The wifely image is rendered attractive through a complex of strategies. A knowing and passive acceptance of a husband's abuse, the symbolism that surrounds the married state, mangalsutra, kumkum, bangles, flowers, the delicious pleasure that women experience when they realize that their self-sacrifice, sorrow and martyrdom grant them an ineffable power over others—all these combine to represent wifedom as a worthy and fulfilling state. Besides, only by being a wife do women obtain a measure of self-possession, composure. Wifedom allows a woman to exercise responsibility and power in her immediate kinship and familial circle—she can plot marriages, negotiate dowries, play an active role in securing her husband's interest within the joint or extended family, anticipate and plan for the even more fulfilling role of motherhood.

We can also see how women are, in fact, prepared for their romantic and conjugal vocations through social rituals and customs. The little girl's sense of her body is informed by a sense of shame; she cannot show her underwear, she must learn to sit with her legs together. As she grows up, she realizes that her body, which she had learnt to hide and guard, is meant for a certain and higher destiny. Puberty rituals mark her coming of age, marking her body in an unmistakable manner, drawing attention to its fertility. These rituals also fill her with a sense of pride. Now she is almost a woman, ready to take her place along with other adult women in her community.

The imperatives to be female and wifely in particular sorts of ways affect women who have different sexual preferences in complex ways. Lesbian love is forced into hiding, and, worse, has to consent to heterosexual practices which come in the wake of marriage. Women who are clear that they do not desire heterosexual marriage have found it hard to construct other sorts of lives for themselves. Very few role models exist and they necessarily live out their lives in shadows. This has led several women to enter into suicide pacts, to run away, contract informal marriage arrangements ('maitri' unions).

Women's experience of motherhood is more complex. Romance and marriage are more clearly and transparently linked to issues of social status and economic security, whereas motherhood is experienced as something intensely personal, pertaining to the individual woman's most intimate sense of herself. Firstly, it is an identifiable female physical condition. A woman bears a child in her womb and it shows. Secondly, motherhood is also an experience that the female body feels in every pore of its corporeal being—so much so that the emotions, feelings and thoughts it evokes are not easily separable from the actual body from which these emanate. It is hardly surprising then that women associate their sense of motherhood and their understanding of it with a natural, given state.

This has several implications. If a woman cannot be a mother, she feels guilty, as if it is her fault, as if her body has betrayed itself and her. Women also imagine that whatever else they are or may do, their ultimate destiny is linked with motherhood. Thus successful, professional women, women who have decided to stay single, women who long to get married and have a child, but who cannot, for whatever reason, at some point in their lives, all of them feel inadequate, unfulfilled and somehow less of a woman. Most women unquestioningly accept that mothering is an exclusive female activity and if they cannot attain that state or do justice to it, though they have attained it, feel they have failed their essential vocation. Working mothers, for instance, experience a sense of utter helplessness when a child falls ill or has failed in her exams—they feel it is their responsibility and these problems could have been averted, had they stayed at home and been good, caring mothers.

On the other hand, motherhood is also a social institution: custom, culture and history do influence women's perceptions and experience of motherhood. For example, in late eighteenth-century France, several urban middle class and lower middle class women, including young working mothers who had come to the city to make a living, used to send their children away to rural wet nurses till they were weaned. These surrogate mothers were paid for their ability to breastfeed these alien children. In this society, being a mother was not central to a woman's sense of herself. She seems to have adopted a rather pragmatic attitude towards the experience.

To consider another example: a different dimension to motherhood existed in eighteenth- and nineteenth-century America. African-American slave women were employed by their white mistresses as wet nurses. Often these women had to neglect their own children or leave them to fend for themselves. African-American children could be beaten and put to work on the great sugar and cotton plantations. In these circumstances, a slave mother had to fight ferociously to prevent her child from being abused. Sometimes she suffered beatings and whips so that her children could be saved from the master's wrath. In certain circumstances, African-American women are known to have killed their children rather than submit them to the cruelty of the white plantation owners.

Clearly, like other institutions that we have created, motherhood too possesses specific social meanings. Yet there are very few moments in history when it was not considered a woman's destiny or vocation. Though different social arrangements existed for the care of children, rarely did these involve men. It was almost as if the child was an extension of the woman's body, her very self, and she or other women had to assume sole and responsible care for it.

How and why did women accept these social arrangements? Partly because many of them were unable to separate their experience of motherhood from the social meanings that had come to be invested in it. But there existed—and these reasons are valid for the present as well—other reasons why women wore this role well and ably. For one, motherhood allows women a measure of agency which wifehood denied them—the children are theirs, to raise as they desire, to feel and coddle, as their own. Secondly, being a mother has its familial and social compensations; her status within the immediate kinship network is enhanced, once she becomes a mother, especially if she has borne a male infant. Literature, social custom and consensus view her as the child's primary teacher and guide.

Across cultures, the mother's role is a dynamic and powerful one. Women have and continue to utilize the power they wield over their children to their advantage. One may argue that this is a pyrrhic sort of power, exercised well within the long shadow of patriarchy: yet in actual life, this power earns rewards and authority. This is especially evident—in the Indian context, at least—in the influence mothers command with grown-up sons, the authority that older women, especially mothers-in-law, enjoy over younger women, and, most important, in the pride with which mothers persuade and entreat their daughters to accept and live out the destinies and vocations which had propelled their own lives.

Most of us are familiar with the image of the domineering and heartless mother-in-law. Indeed many of us concerned with questions of women's rights and freedom are often asked to account for the 'fact' that women are women's worst enemies. This observation annoys us, makes us impatient with the interlocutor, often a man, but in many instances, women as well. Usually, we are likely to respond, a trifle bitterly, that such conflicts are to be expected in a patriarchal social order where women's power is a pale reflection of the real power wielded by men. But clearly this does not explain or help the truly confused make sense of the vicious and deeply felt jealousy and anxiety contained in the mother-in-law's attitude towards her son's young bride. Afraid of losing her place in her son's life, helpless before the curious and happy sexuality of the young woman, determined to put to use a power that has eluded her when she was young, and which is now hers, the mother-in-law is not merely a victim of a system, but also one of its constituent elements. This power is directed not only at the young wife but also at the son. He, for his part, has to establish his primordial loyalties to his mother, while negotiating an independent conjugal life for himself.

Less familiar and understood, but equally ubiquitous is the mother's role in her daughter's life. The mother schools her female child into a disciplinary regime, involving the body, emotions, the mind and consciousness. In most cultures, and in India especially, it is the mother who instils in the girl child a sense of her difference. She does this, firstly, by carefully covering her genitalia. As the child grows, she is watchful of her development, she admonishes her, were she to sit or stand in a particular way. She makes sure the little girl is dressed daintily, prettily. She teaches the child to regard housework as legitimately hers. By the time the child is self-aware, she knows that as a girl, she must never do anything to attract shameful attention, that she should guard her body, and learn to be patient, quiet and await her turn. When she attains puberty, the mother is both excited and afraid; happy that the girl is now ready for her destiny, worried that now her 'maidenhood' has to be carefully protected until she is handed over to the further and ultimate protection of her husband. The point is the mother repeats and replays the various little feminine dramas that had informed her own childhood and adolescence in her daughter's life, almost gleeful that the state of subordination in which she had lived is not hers alone anymore.

Again, as with notions of beauty, the experiences of femininity have been thoroughly criticized and re-interpreted by feminists. Feminists have stressed on women's right to sexual pleasure, challenged the submissive role assigned to the wife, declared that motherhood ought to be enabling and empowering rather than restricting and limiting. Likewise, radical female homosexuals, some of whom are active in the women's movements, have flaunted their experiences of both gender and sexuality as proof that there is nothing given about women's roles, their bodily functions.

Masculine Lives

Masculinity connotes and invites emotions and acts which affirm the male self from which they emerge. Unlike the paired sexual ideal that informs women's sense of themselves, their sexuality and their destinies, ideal maleness does not respond to an outside gaze. Instead, it is defined by the power to look, assess, judge, measure and act. A little boy who dashes up a tree, while his sister hovers uncertainly on the ground; an older man plunges into a life of adventure and travel, while his wife or mother anxiously wait at home, hoping and praying for his safety. Men are confident, act as if it is given to them to do so, as if the entire world is theirs for the taking. While economic power, educational advantages and the familial and social roles they play inspire this easy confidence, this latter is always an embodied quality. That is, it marks a man's experiences and expressions of his body—both in relationship to others and to the world in which he lives.

If women's bodies are to please and be pleasing, men's bodies are expected to be expressive of a certain innate rude energy. Physical exercise, hard work, a healthy sexual appetite are taken to be typical male attributes and acts. If a man shuns any of the above, it is usually because he does so in the service of a higher and ostensibly loftier aim, such as the pursuit of truth or God. The dictum to men to be tough and energetic in turn creates its own specific anxieties and obsessions. While women are anxious to draw attention and feel doomed if they do not, men press themselves upon the world and women, insistently making their presence felt through a loud tone of voice, firm footsteps, gestures that enable them effortlessly to colonize a room, a hall. This desire to be present in everything they do and say renders men narcissistic in the extreme. For the most part, they remain oddly opaque to a world that is not imprinted with their image, be it the nursery or the intimate inner world of emotions and relationships.

Men rarely however, see themselves thus: as bounded and hemmed in by their own selves and drives. Since they perceive themselves to be actors and agents, people who make things happen, they experience neither a sense of lack nor do they feel particularly inadequate. When they do feel either of these emotions, they are palpably handicapped, either physically slight and feminine, or impotent or simply sexually disabled.

Homosexual men, though, realize all too well, the limits to masculinity. They also know and experience first-hand, the pressures of being male. For these work to their disadvantage and, worse, prove oppressive. This is visible in instances of homosexual-bashing in parts of the United States of America, for example. But the criminalization of homosexuals and the tacit insistence that they conform to 'normal' masculine standards happen even in India. There are provisions in the Indian Penal Code which can and are used to harass and intimidate homosexual men.

What does it mean for a man to see himself as an agent, to experience initiative and dynamism? How do these sensibilities translate into expressive action? Generally speaking, a man attempts to affirm his sense of existence through the following means; his sexual character and appetite; his familial power; his status as the head of the household; his position in the outside world of work, peers; in terms of his relationship to authority. Let us consider each of these in turn. A man's relationship to sexuality, his body, his sexual needs, and desires is inextricably linked with his sense of his own importance as a superior human being whose appetites are natural, a sign of well-being. Hence his body becomes an instrument of performance.

Thus, whether he is exercising, grooming himself, or even attending to more mundane tasks, such as urinating on the road or boarding a running bus, he seeks to flaunt his maleness. He displays in each instance, his sense of physical prowess, charm, his ability to claim public space as his own, his dare-devilry.

Or consider that oddly named phenomenon: eve-teasing. It is perhaps the most perfect example of how a young man views himself and others, in this case, women, and his relationship to the immediate environment. He wolf-whistles at women, sings out lines from a well-chosen bawdy song, calls out obscene riddles, sometimes stalks the woman in question, lying in wait for her, even delighting in her horror, fear, her dread and anticipation of his presence. These acts express a self, a body that needs to harass and instil fear and humiliation in an unknown woman to even express its sexual emotion. The person of the woman does not matter, neither do her emotions, the fact that these things take place in a public context is of no consequence because for men, the world outside is their own, an almost marked territory. If women trespass, they must do so at their own peril. A desire to torment sits deliciously closely to a need thus to affirm one's maleness.

A sense of bravura, of power that delights in its ability to trouble others, especially women, gratuitously and pointlessly, enable men to wed love, even romantic love to violence. This could be the insidious violence of the chase, the hunt that pursues its quarry relentlessly, forcing it to yield at a point where the victim of the chase, feels near relief at not having to run anymore and is willing to surrender herself to a romance that means to devour her. This is a situation that ought to be all too familiar to us from our daily film fare. In other instances, men demonstrate love in a combative fashion: to possess and win a woman at any cost and to wrest her away from another man, once again, to demand her undying loyalty and affection through sheer persistence. This is of course high romance, cultivated in pulp fiction and forming the stuff of romantic commonsense among youthful girls. There is another sort of violent love, where beating, abuse, jealousy and suspicion, a desire to seek out the beloved, only to hurt her, all have their place. This is more commonly found within institutionalized relationships, especially marriage. In all these instances, a man's attempts at loving is deeply intertwined with his need to establish his control over the romance, the body of the young woman, and underscore his possession of the latter.

Psychological reasons—such as those adduced by Dinnerstein and Kakar—may help us make sense of men's need to dominate and control. The material and social basis for this domination are, however, quite clear. Men's ability to exercise control over women's sexuality and male access to productive resources define their familial duties and their functions and roles in the outside world. Unlike women to whom marriage is the only legitimate avenue to companionship and sexual intimacy, for men, marriage is a social arrangement that services their sexual and emotional needs, without actually containing them. Besides, marriage helps him secure those conditions necessary for him to fan out into the world: to farm, work, sell, travel, intellectualize, and so on.

Fatherhood is neither an arduous task nor a responsibility for a man, on the other hand it grants him the authority to mark his children as his own. They are known by his name, will inherit from him and preserve his name in future. Men do not worry about children in an obsessive sort of way. Child-care happens, is part of the natural, organic female universe, where growth, nurture, and tending are to be expected. If the glory of motherhood is expounded in song, custom and literature, fatherhood enjoys a significant status in law, matters of the state—almost all government forms in India require us to fill in the name of the father. The status of a father is thus both biological and secular: as a father a man partakes of a civil identity. A father is the head of the household in most countries, most property documents exist in his name, his children are known by his patronymic. This civil identity places him in two worlds: the familial and the social. Motherhood on the other hand possesses no civil status and remains locked within the familial sphere of home, babies, nurture.

In turn, it may be said, it is the power that men wield in the outside world, as owners of property, managers of resources and workers, which grants their fatherly identity such civil significance. As we have seen, the authority of men came to prevail gradually, whether this was due to their control over female sexuality and labour, or their possession of productive resources or both. Male authority when it arrived and crystallized into its familiar forms, rooted itself in the spheres of reproduction as well as production.

At this point in our argument, we once again need to qualify the category 'men'. Not all men seek to possess or possess either the chance or the power to express their sexual energy, their will to authority. Poor men, men condemned to various forms of untouchability, disabled men, men of low social status—all of these are bound to an economics of survival and dependence. In this context, the imperative to be male, virile and in control can only seem ironic. On the other hand, as I have pointed out elsewhere, with reference to dalit men, even powerless men possess sexual authority, power over women's bodies, even if this is only within the space of their homes.

NORMS OF THE BODY

Beauty and virility, the experience of romance, the state of marriage, motherhood and fatherhood: these are produced and actualized in society through a complex of institutions and individuals. Among these are modes of dress, child-rearing practices, rites of passage that attend the onset of puberty in girls (and in some cases, of boys as well), social rituals that impress upon boys and girls their respective vocations (these are varied), everyday living in the course of which food, education, entertainment and leisure are allocated differently to boys and girls. Also included are the world of production which demands differently weighted tasks for boys and girls, the sphere of reproduction, which includes housework, child-care, care of the old and the sick, tasks which are clearly for girls, cultural codes, songs, stories, films, all of which uphold distinctive gender attributes and destinies. All these in association with each other create the conditions in which girls grow up, wanting to be beautiful and chaste, and boys, confident and virile.

These various social practices reach us through relationships: parents, peers, teachers, friends, a variety of people figure in the drama of growing up female or male. They exercise their influence on our bodies, minds, emotions and souls. But this does not happen through threats, coercive rules or the handing out of punishment. We act out, take in, embody these various injunctions. They figure in, are demonstrated through the relationships we live as mothers and fathers, wives and husbands, teenage girls and boys. Consequently, we do not view these various practices that direct us as coming from outside. As far as we are concerned, they constitute the very stuff of life and grant it form, direction and meaning.

Are we or are we not, then, victims of a system of power that cunningly controls our each and every movement? Not really. We are not passive recipients of messages, we decode them, express them through our emotional and ethical choices and preferences. Let us take the paired female ideal. We actualize it in any number of ways: by buying into the beauty myth, by actively taking against women known for their fierce independence or sexual daring, by endorsing the myth of the self-sacrificing wife. We counsel friends who are in an unhappy marriage to 'somehow adjust', We convince ourselves and other women that the female of the species cannot seriously contemplate a life of solitude.

Or as men we practise double standards: demand monogamous loyalty from wives and girlfriends, while reserving for ourselves the right to philander. More generally, men tend to control and regulate the sexuality of those women who are within the familial network, while remaining appreciative and lustful of female promiscuity directed at them from outside the family.

Of course, both men and women flout norms, refuse to fall in line, yet everywhere they come up against real limits. A spunky woman who stands up bravely to sexual harassment, who refuses to remain demure and passive in the face of provocation finds out, sooner or later, that ultimately the streets are not safe for her, she also comes up against ingrained prejudices. People are wont to blame her for being forward and unfeminine. To her dismay she finds out that the law is not in her favour, and even if it is, it is interpreted by men who do not look kindly upon female freedom. Most important, she realizes that she does not possess the mobility and ease to feel entirely comfortable in public spaces, where she is made to feel uneasy, viewed as an illegitimate presence. It is as if she is being told that she belongs to the inner world, of home and family. The point is individuals may bend the norms to their advantage, but these norms do not bend all the way. There are limits that hold them back.

These limits are all too visible even in those instances, where the norm appears to have vanished. Take the case of men who wish to share housework and parenting, who are not self-conscious about being 'feminine'. Such men clearly have sought to distinguish themselves from an aggressive and imperious masculinity. Yet very few of these 'feminine' men who have broken the gender line will settle for lesser wages, a semi-literate education and a low-status job. All attempts to be 'different' often collapse in the face of material interests and concerns.

The limits to rule-breaking constitute the outermost contours of a social system which we shall describe as patriarchy, keeping in mind the diverse interpretations of this system. These limits have to do with the material life lead by men and women and the roles and functions that are supposed to be innate to them. Thus, whatever interpretation we choose, it is clear that under patriarchy, women, whose lives are defined by reproduction and familial responsibilities, find themselves 'blocked' out of many experiences: for example, the freedom of the outdoors, a life of adventure, professions that require travel and mobility. Women also find it less easy to change their lives mid-way, should they desire it. For they are considered 'settled'—once they are married and have children, it is assumed life cannot be wanting in any respect. There are, of course, exceptions, but these are truly so.

Education and work enhance a woman's chances; to travel, newer friendships. Yet these chances are limited because women rarely imagine they deserve these things. They suffer guilt, should they utilize a holiday to get away somewhere on their own, wonder if they should have not involved the entire family in their travel plans. It may be said that women are convinced that experiences that lie beyond the ken of the family and the larger kinship network are not legitimate. Nor is the world so arranged that they can venture forth thus, without having to suffer guilt for it. Child-care, housework, kinship obligations—all these combine to render her world limited and closed. While matters have changed for educated, middle class women, their world continues to remain bounded. Their domestic and kinship responsibilities do not grow any less, simply because they have other things to do. They remain as tied to notions of traditional femininity as other women. There are, of course, kinds of inaccessibility. For instance, poorer women are more mobile, because of the nature of their work, but have fewer choices when it comes to education.

On the whole, men do not suffer from similar blockage, but their sense of themselves and the positions they occupy render them strangers to emotions and intimacies. While lack of access to experiences and resources work to women's disadvantage, men utilize their alienation from certain experiences to underscore their authority.

SUMMING UP

It is clear that norms of control lie at the very core of practices of gender. In the first instance, these norms are held in place by social and economic structures which determine a person's access to resources, culture and power. As we pointed out in the first chapter, men and women live out these norms, in the context of these structures, sometimes working against their grain, at other times, within the terms of their logic—but always performing roles, identities, fulfilling functions and expectations. This system of norms, structure and individual performances of norms together create a social order we recognize as patriarchal. Patriarchy, however, is not merely a regulated system, it is also the world we live in, embodied in the ways we eat, dress, speak, love and die.

Of the several elements which constitute patriarchy, gender is perhaps the most significant, because it allows for the articulation of power within relationships that are fundamental and intimate. In this sense, gender is not merely an ordering principle, a basis from which to understand how men and women came to be what they are today, but also a relationship. This relationship of the two sexes, mediated by ideas and structures, organizes our world in particular and hierarchical ways. Gender is thus not merely a methodological category but a way of signifying relationships of power.

Conclusion

We have tried to discuss the phenomenon of gender. The observations and arguments of the preceding chapters have attempted to demonstrate that gender is an aspect of our everyday lives as well as a social, economic and cultural category that subsumes and re-writes the meaning of human sex, the fact of being masculine and feminine.

The book has emphasized thoroughout that identities, roles and relationships that are associated with gender have come about as a result of human agency. That is, they are neither innate, nor given, but constructed, made and re-made by human beings as they lived, worked, loved and procreated. Through an examination of male and female relationships in diverse fields, from sexuality to economics, the arguments in this book have drawn attention to a crucial fact: gender norms that regulate male and female behaviour may be traced back to a very important historical development: the relegation of women to the realms of sexuality, reproduction and mothering.

We have also tried to grapple consistently with the question of women's subjectivity and agency. Are women victims of patriarchal systems or are they partial collaborators? Why do women wear the marks of their subordination, their imposed inferiority with such pride? Instead of viewing patriarchal power as merely limiting and restrictive, the book suggests that this power, in fact, is productive. It has created the familial and social worlds that we know, are familiar with, and which shape our selfhood. Further, it is a world that women have helped to make, though they participate on unequal terms and for questionable returns.

One of the more intriguing questions that this book raises has to do with the tenacity of gender norms. How have they survived and why? Even if we are to admit that at some time in the distant past, women's reproductive functions were deemed important, why should it continue to define and influence subsequent perceptions of women? The book's responses to these concerns are brief but immensely suggestive: the subordination of women did not happen as a singular event. Women, slaves, the so-called untouchables and working people were all equally subjected to a social and economic system of exploitation and oppression. Gender is a crucial node in the creation of power, but it is not the only one. Economic and class power, religious authority, sexual norms, brute force, or a combination of all of these worked to create patriarchal systems.

Finally we have drawn attention to the fact that gender is a lived and experienced relationship of power and love, authority and intimacy. It has shown that radical critiques of gender are as concerned with re-making human relationships, transforming our notions of sexual love and companionship, as they are with challenging economic and social hierarchy.

In conclusion, it may be said that understanding gender is a task that is both easy and slippery. It is easy because we are doing gender all the time, and it is all around us. It is slippery because it has to do with our sense of ourselves, our roles and relationships. We are liable to practise self-deception and justify personal choices, fantasize, employ arguments to our personal advantage. Yet there is no way to take stock except through this process of questioning, both the self and the world. Such a questioning is neither easy nor pleasant. It involves re-learning things we take for granted: voice, gesture, body language, speech, to name a few. It also requires that we step past easy sentiment, pat responses and sloganistic solutions.

This book, however, does not offer prescriptions for understanding. It provides a critical context to enable us to understand and evaluate the choices we make as women and men, and to interpret and understand them. In this sense, the book has merely sketched in the contours of knowing, it is the reader who has to complete the process of comprehending and relating what she has read to her life, its immediate context and the larger world.

Bibliography

INTRODUCTION

My understanding of gender as both an object and category of analysis owes a great deal to the following works:

Connell, Robert, *Gender and Power*, Cambridge: Polity Press, 1997.

Scott, Joan W, 'Gender'. In *Coming to Terms: Feminism, Theory, Politics*, edited by Elizabeth Weed, New York: Routledge, 1989.

CHAPTER 1

The explanations and arguments in this chapter are drawn from a range of sources, and the most important ones are listed.

The following books helped to formulate the arguments in the section on religion.

Chakravarti, Uma, 'Conceptualising Brahminical Patriarchy in Early India: Gender, Caste, Class and State', *Economic and Political Weekly* (henceforth EPW) (3 April 1993).

Ganesh, Kamala, 'Mother Who Is Not a Mother: In Search of the Great Indian Mother Goddess', EPW (20-27 October 1990).

Gimbutas, Marjia, *The Gods and Goddesses of Old Europe*, Berkeley, CA: University of California Press, 1974.

Manushi, special ed on Women Bhakti Poets, nos 50, 51, 52 1989.

Warner, Marina, *Alone of All Her Sex: The Myth and Cult of the Virgin Mary*, New York: Vintage, 1983.
Yamani, Mai, *Feminism and Islam: Legal and Literary Perspectives*, Reading, Berkshire: Ithaca Press with Garnett Publishing, 1996.

On science and gender, I found the following books most useful:

Bleier, Ruth, *Science and Gender*, New York: Oxford University Press, 1984.
Fausto-Sterling, Anne, *Myths of Gender, Biological Theories about Men and Women*, New York: Basic Books, 1985.
Keller, Evelyn Fox, *Reflections on Gender and Science*, New Haven: Yale University Press, 1985.
Schiebinger, Londa, *Has Feminism Changed Science?* Cambridge, Ma: Harvard University Press, 1999.
Wertheim, Margaret, *Pythagoras' Trousers: God, Physics and the Gender Wars*, London: Fourth Estate, 1997.

My observations on *women, politics and modern democracy* were largely influenced by that classic work, on women in movements, Sheila Rowbotham, *Feminism and Social Action*, New York: Routledge, 1992.

CHAPTERS 2-4

These interlinked chapters base their arguments on a set of theses outlined by Robert Connell in *Gender and Power*. I give details of chapters from the book that proved useful. I also include books that helped me in working through these arguments.

Connell, Robert, 'Historical Roots of Contemporary Theory'. In *Gender and Power*, Cambridge: Polity Press, 1987.
——, 'Current Fameworks'. In *Gender and Power*, Cambridge: Polity Press, 1987.
de Beavoir, Simone, *The Second Sex*, New York: Knopf, 1953.
Gilligan, Carol, *In a Different Voice: Psychological Theory and Women's Development*, Cambridge, Ma: Harvard University Press, 1993.
Harding, Sandra, *The Science Question in Feminism*, Ithaca: Cornell University Press, 1986.
Lerner, Gerda *The Creation of Feminist Consciousness*, New York:

Oxford University Press, 1993.
Moore, Henrietta L., *Feminism and Anthropology*, Cambridge: Polity Press, 1988.
Scott, Joan W. *Gender and the Politics of History*, New York: Columbia University Press, 1988.

CHAPTER 5

Each of the subsections in this chapter deserve a comprehensive bibliographical note. I give here only the most often cited works.

On *Friedrich Engels and the World-Historic Defeat of the Female Sex*

Boulding, Elise, *The Underside of History: A View of Women Through Time*, Boulder: Westview Press, 1976.
Engels, Freidrich, *The Origin of the Family, Private Property and the State*. Moscow: Progress Publishers, 1948.
Levi-Strauss, C., *The Elementary Structures of Kinship*, London: Tavistock, 1969.
Meillassoux, Claude, *Maidens, Meal and Money*, Cambridge: Cambridge University Press, 1981.
Mitchell, Juliet, 'Women: The Longest Revolution'. In *Women's Estate*, New York: Pantheon, 1971.
Sacks, Karen, 'Engels Re-visited: Women, the Organisation of Production and Private Property'. In *Woman, Culture and Society*, edited by M. Rosaldo and L. Lamphere, Stanford: Stanford University Press, 1974.

On *The Creation of Patriarchy*

Boulding, Elise, *The Underside of History: A View of Women Through Time*, Boulder: Westview, 1976.
Lerner, Gerda, *The Creation of Patriarchy*, New York: Oxford University Press, 1986.

On *Becoming Men and Women; With Freud and After Him*

Dinnerstein, Dorothy, *The Mermaid and the Minotaur: Sexual Arrangements and the Human Malaise*, New York: Harper and Row, 1976.
Freud, Sigmund, *Three Essays on the Theory of Sexuality, Complete Psychological Works*, vol. 7, London: Hogarth, 1953.
—, *Civilisation and Its Discontents*, Complete Psychological

Works, vol. 21, London: Hogarth, 1961.
Gilbert, Harriet, ed., *The Sexual Imagination from Acker to Zolla: A Feminist Companion*, London: Cape, 1993.
Horney, Karen, *Feminine Psychology*, London: Routledge and Kegan Paul, 1967.
Harding, Esther M., *Women's Mysteries: Ancient and Modern*, New York: Harper Colophon, 1976.
Jung, Carl G., *The Relations between the Ego and the Unconscious*, Collected Works, vol. 7, London: Routledge and Kegan Paul, 1953.
Kakar, Sudhir, *The Inner World*, Delhi: Oxford University Press, 1989.
Kristeva, Julia, *Revolution in Poetic Language*, New York: Columbia University Press, 1984.
Lacan, Jacques, *The Four Fundamental Concepts of Psychoanalysis*, New York: Norton, 1981.

On *Against Our Will*
Brownmiller, Susan, *Against Our Will, Men: Women and Rape*, New York, Simon and Schuster, 1975.
Dworkin, Andrea, *Pornography: Men Possessing Women*, New York: Putnam, 1981.
MacKinnon, Catharine, *Feminism Reconsidered*, Cambridge, Ma: Harvard University Press, 1987.
Rich, Adrienne, *Compulsory Heterosexuality and Lesbian Identity*, London: Only Women Press, 1981.
Schneir, Miriam, ed., *The Vintage Book of Feminism*, New York: Vintage, 1995.
Steinem, Gloria, 'What If Freud Were Phyllis?' in *Moving Beyond Words*, edited by Gloria Steinem, New York: Simon and Schuster, 1994.

On *Understanding History*
This section draws on published works and also the author's own memories of the women's movements: the debates and arguments around the question of gender and sexuality that emerged within the practice of these movements.

On *Periyar: Property, Caste and Gender*
The observations and argument in this section are drawn from:

V. Geetha, and S.V. Rajadurai, *Towards a Non-Brahmin Millennium: From Iyothee Thass to Periyar*, Calcutta: Samya, 1998; rev ed, 2008; rpt 2011.

On *Understanding Brahminical Patriarchy*
Chakravarti, Uma, 'Conceptualising Brahminical Patriarchy in Early India, Gender, Caste, Class and State', *EPW* (3 April 1993).
—, *The Life and Times of Pandita Ramabhai,* Delhi: Kali for Women, 1998.
Chowdhury, Prem, *The Veiled Woman: Shifting Gender Equations in Rural Haryana,* Delhi: Oxford University Press, 1994.

On *Sexuality and Subordination*
Agnes, Flavia, *My Story, Our Story, Building Broken Lives,* Mumbai: Forum Against Oppression of Women, 1984. rpt. 1988.
Kannabiran, Vasanth, and Kannabiran, Kalpana, 'Caste and Gender: Understanding the Dynamic of Power and Violence', *EPW* (14 September 1991).
Omvedt, Gail, *Violence Against Women: New Movements and New Theories in India,* Delhi: Kali for Women, 1990.

CHAPTER 6

This last chapter is necessarily impressionistic and suggestive. It comprises loud and suggestive thinking on several interlinked issues that have been central to feminist politics in India and elsewhere.

Index